# Educational Leadership and Policy in a Time of Precarity

This book brings critical perspectives towards questions of how precarity and precarious ness affect the work of leaders and educators in schools and universities around the worl It theorises the effects of precarity and the experiences of educators working in precariou environments.

The work of school improvement takes time. Developing a highly skilled and confide teaching workforce requires a long-term investment and commitment. Schools in vulnerab communities face higher rates of turnover and difficulty in staffing than advantaged schoc do. Tackling the big issues in education – inequity, opportunity gaps, democracy and c hesion – also takes time. Education systems and sectors around the globe are functioni in increasingly casualised workforce environments, which has implications for leadersh in schools and in higher education institutions. Precarity also holds serious implicatic for policymakers and for the leaders and educators who have to enact those policies. T book brings together experts in the field to offer critical perspectives on questions of h we might theorise the effects of precarity and the experiences of those people working precarious environments.

*Educational Leadership and Policy in a Time of Precarity* will be a key resource for a demics; researchers; and advanced students of education leadership and policy, educatio administration, research methods and sociology. This book was originally published a special issue of the *Journal of Educational Administration and History*.

**Amanda Heffernan** is Senior Lecturer in Educational Leadership at the Manchester In tute of Education at the University of Manchester, UK.

**Jane Wilkinson** is Professor of Educational Leadership at the Faculty of Education Monash University, Melbourne, Australia

# Educational Leadership and Policy in a Time of Precarity

*Edited by*
Amanda Heffernan and Jane Wilkinson

LONDON AND NEW YORK

First published 2024
by Routledge
4 Park Square, Milton Park, Abingdon, Oxon, OX14 4RN

and by Routledge
605 Third Avenue, New York, NY 10158

*Routledge is an imprint of the Taylor & Francis Group, an informa business*

© 2024 Taylor & Francis

All rights reserved. No part of this book may be reprinted or reproduced or utilised in any form or by any electronic, mechanical, or other means, now known or hereafter invented, including photocopying and recording, or in any information storage or retrieval system, without permission in writing from the publishers.

*Trademark notice*: Product or corporate names may be trademarks or registered trademarks, and are used only for identification and explanation without intent to infringe.

*British Library Cataloguing-in-Publication Data*
A catalogue record for this book is available from the British Library

ISBN13: 978-1-032-58818-6 (hbk)
ISBN13: 978-1-032-58819-3 (pbk)
ISBN13: 978-1-003-45161-7 (ebk)

DOI: 10.4324/9781003451617

Typeset in Minion Pro
by codeMantra

**Publisher's Note**
The publisher accepts responsibility for any inconsistencies that may have arisen during the conversion of this book from journal articles to book chapters, namely the inclusion of journal terminology.

**Disclaimer**
Every effort has been made to contact copyright holders for their permission to reprint material in this book. The publishers would be grateful to hear from any copyright holder who is not here acknowledged and will undertake to rectify any errors or omissions in future editions of this book.

# Contents

| | | |
|---|---|---|
| *Citation Information* | | vii |
| *Notes on Contributors* | | ix |

Introduction—Educational leadership and policy: precarity
and precariousness    1
*Amanda Heffernan and Jane Wilkinson*

1   Theorising and preparing students for precarity: how can leaders and
educators better prepare students to enter an increasingly
insecure workforce?    7
*Lucas Walsh and Joanne Gleeson*

2   Creative industries curriculum design for living and
leading amid uncertainty    20
*Gail Crimmins, Briony Lipton, Joanna McIntyre, Margarietha de Villiers
Scheepers and Peter English*

3   Ethical responsibilities of tenured academics supervising non-tenured
researchers in times of neoliberalism and precarity    37
*Kathleen Smithers, Jess Harris, Mhorag Goff, Nerida Spina and Simon Bailey*

4   Teachers, fixed-term contracts and school leadership: toeing the line and
jumping through hoops    54
*Meghan Stacey, Scott Fitzgerald, Rachel Wilson, Susan McGrath-Champ and
Mihajla Gavin*

5   Embracing vulnerability: how has the Covid-19 pandemic affected the
pressures school leaders in Northern England face and
how they deal with them?    69
*Michael Jopling and Oliver Harness*

6   Repositioned professionals and heterodox: a response to the precarity of
reform in further education    85
*Lewis Entwistle*

# CONTENTS

7 Necessary risk: addressing precarity by re-envisioning teaching
and learning                                                    105
*Jeanne M. Powers and Lok-Sze Wong*

*Index*                                                          121

# Citation Information

The chapters in this book were originally published in the *Journal of Educational Administration and History*, volume 54, issue 1 (2022). When citing this material, please use the original page numbering for each article, as follows:

**Introduction**
*Educational Leadership and Policy: Precarity and Precariousness*
Amanda Heffernan and Jane Wilkinson
*Journal of Educational Administration and History*, volume 54, issue 1 (2022) pp. 1–6

**Chapter 1**
*Theorising and Preparing Students for Precarity: How can leaders and educators better prepare students to enter an increasingly insecure workforce?*
Lucas Walsh and Joanne Gleeson
*Journal of Educational Administration and History*, volume 54, issue 1 (2022) pp. 7–19

**Chapter 2**
*Creative industries curriculum design for living and leading amid uncertainty*
Gail Crimmins, Briony Lipton, Joanna McIntyre, Margarietha de Villiers Scheepers and Peter English
*Journal of Educational Administration and History*, volume 54, issue 1 (2022) pp. 20–36

**Chapter 3**
*Ethical responsibilities of tenured academics supervising non-tenured researchers in times of neoliberalism and precarity*
Kathleen Smithers, Jess Harris, Mhorag Goff, Nerida Spina and Simon Bailey
*Journal of Educational Administration and History*, volume 54, issue 1 (2022) pp. 37–53

**Chapter 4**
*Teachers, fixed-term contracts and school leadership: toeing the line and jumping through hoops*
Meghan Stacey, Scott Fitzgerald, Rachel Wilson, Susan McGrath-Champ and Mihajla Gavin
*Journal of Educational Administration and History*, volume 54, issue 1 (2022) pp. 54–68

viii CITATION INFORMATION

## Chapter 5

*Embracing vulnerability: how has the Covid-19 pandemic affected the pressures school leaders in Northern England face and how they deal with them?*
Michael Jopling and Oliver Harness
*Journal of Educational Administration and History,* volume 54, issue 1 (2022) pp. 69–84

## Chapter 6

*Repositioned professionals and heterodox: a response to the precarity of reform in further education*
Lewis Entwistle
*Journal of Educational Administration and History,* volume 54, issue 1 (2022) pp. 85–104

## Chapter 7

*Necessary risk: addressing precarity by re-envisioning teaching and learning*
Jeanne M. Powers and Lok-Sze Wong
*Journal of Educational Administration and History,* volume 54, issue 1 (2022) pp. 105–120

For any permission-related enquiries please visit:
http://www.tandfonline.com/page/help/permissions

# Notes on Contributors

**Simon Bailey** is Research Fellow at the Centre for Health Services Studies at the University of Kent, UK. His interests are in the sociological study of technology, work and organisation, with a recent focus upon precarious and project-based work.

**Gail Crimmins** is Deputy Head (L&T) at the School of Business and Creative Industries at the University of the Sunshine Coast, Australia. Her research interests include gender equity, diversity and inclusion, and graduate employability in universities.

**Margarietha de Villiers Scheepers** is Senior Lecturer of Entrepreneurship and Innovation at the School of Business and Creative Industries at the University of the Sunshine Coast, Australia. Her research and teaching focuses on entrepreneurial decision-making, innovation processes and employability.

**Peter English** is Senior Lecturer at the University of the Sunshine Coast, Australia. His main research area is sports journalism, but he also focuses on broader journalism, media and education topics.

**Lewis Entwistle** works in Further Education and completed his EdD in 2019 at the University of Manchester, UK. His research interests are in policy scholarship, education leadership and professional participation.

**Scott Fitzgerald** is Associate Professor at the School of Management and Marketing at Curtin Business School at Curtin University, Perth, Australia. His research interests are located in the broad areas of industrial relations, human resource management, organisational behaviour and organisation studies.

**Mihajla Gavin** is Lecturer at UTS Business School, Australia. Her current research focuses on the restructuring of teachers' work and conditions of work, worker voice, and women and employment relations.

**Joanne Gleeson** is Research Fellow at the Faculty of Education at Monash University, Melbourne, Australia. Joanne draws from cross-sectoral professional experience in executive human resource management, business consulting, careers counselling, education and education research.

**Mhorag Goff** is Research Associate at the Centre for Primary Care at the University of Manchester, UK. Her research interests are in STS approaches to health information systems and data, ethnographic research and ethical themes in particular.

# NOTES ON CONTRIBUTORS

**Oliver Harness** is Honorary Research Fellow at the University of Wolverhampton, UK, and Senior School Improvement Adviser. He has a particular interest in school leadership, head teacher well-being and education policy.

**Jess Harris** is Associate Professor at the Teachers and Teaching Research Centre at the School of Education at the University of Newcastle, Australia. She has a specific interest in qualitative research methods and social relationships in educational settings.

**Amanda Heffernan** is Senior Lecturer in Educational Leadership at the Manchester Institute of Education at the University of Manchester, UK.

**Michael Jopling** is Professor of Education and Director of the Education Observatory at the University of Wolverhampton, UK. His research interests centre on working with schools on areas such as educational leadership, school and multi-agency collaboration, education policy and social justice.

**Briony Lipton** is Postdoctoral Research Associate at the University of Sydney Business School, Australia, and Visiting Research Fellow in the Australia and New Zealand School of Government in the ANU Crawford School, Australia. Her research focuses on the gendered dimensions of academic life for women in Australian universities, gender equality and the future of work, and the relationship between the policy and practice.

**Susan McGrath-Champ** is Professor of Work and Employment Relations at the University of Sydney Business School, Australia. Her research extends perspectives on education studies to understand schools as workplaces and learning places, in addition to research on global mobility and crisis management, and the labour and spatial dimensions of global production networks.

**Joanna McIntyre** is Lecturer in Media Studies and Course Director of the Bachelor of Media and Communication in the Department of Media and Communication at the Swinburne University of Technology, Melbourne, Australia. Her research interests include queer and transgender representation, celebrity, film, television and Australian culture.

**Jeanne M. Powers** is Professor in the Mary Lou Fulton Teachers College at Arizona State University, Tempe, USA. Her research agenda is oriented around issues of equity and access in education policy. Recent projects focus on school segregation, school choice and the implementation of complex education reforms.

**Kathleen Smithers** is Research Assistant at the Teachers and Teaching Research Centre at the University of Newcastle, Australia. Her research focuses on equity in all her projects, and her doctoral thesis investigates development tourism in schools in Zimbabwe.

**Nerida Spina** is Senior Lecturer at the Queensland University of Technology, Australia. Her research interests centre around the sociology of numbers, education policy, social justice and equity.

**Meghan Stacey** is Lecturer in the Sociology of Education and Education Policy at the School of Education at UNSW Sydney, Australia. Her research interests include the marketisation of education; teachers' work and workload; and how teachers' work is shaped in relation to, and by, policy.

**Lucas Walsh** is Professor of Education Policy and Practice, Youth Studies, at the Faculty of Education at Monash University, Melbourne, Australia. He is Co-chief Investigator on The Q Project to improve the use of research evidence in schools.

**Jane Wilkinson** is Professor of Educational Leadership at the Faculty of Education at Monash University, Melbourne, Australia.

**Rachel Wilson** is Associate Professor at the School of Education at the University of Sydney, Australia. She has particular expertise in educational assessment, research methods and programme evaluation, with broad interests across educational evidence, policy and practice.

**Lok-Sze Wong** studies system reform policies as attempts to address systemic inequities. She focuses on professional learning opportunities that support teachers and administrators as they shift their practices while redesigning the very organisations in which they work. Dr Wong began her career in education as an elementary school teacher in Los Angeles, USA.

INTRODUCTION

# Educational leadership and policy: precarity and precariousness

Amanda Heffernan ⓘ and Jane Wilkinson ⓘ

> Precarious situations and events are like rugged terrains: every step must be carefully pre-conceived and decisively taken and, even then, one can never be certain that s/he has firm ground under his or her feet.
>
> (della Porta et al. 2015, 3)

This special issue brings a range of perspectives to explore questions of the connections between notions of precarity and education. Authors in this issue explore the myriad ways precarity affects educational leaders and how precarity and education policy are intertwined broadly.

The issue was first conceptualised in 2019 in response to ongoing concerns about precarious employment in education - casualised academia in higher education, increasing reports of short-term teaching contracts, and performance-based contracts for school leaders. Education systems and sectors around the globe are functioning in increasingly casualised workforce environments, which has implications for leadership in schools and in higher education institutions. Precarity also holds serious implications for policy-makers and for the leaders and educators who have to enact those policies.

We know, for example, that the work of school improvement takes time. Developing a highly-skilled and confident teaching workforce requires a long-term investment and commitment. Schools in vulnerable communities face higher rates of turnover and difficulty in staffing. Tackling the big issues in education – inequity, opportunity gaps, democracy and cohesion – also takes time. How are precarious leaders, or leaders in precarious organisations, able to make long-term plans to address these challenges?

The rise of the gig economy also holds significant implications for young people today, and how education is preparing them for an uncertain future. This is not new by any means and Lee and Kofman (2012, 389) describe precarious employment as 'not just the outcome of an inexorable, almost mechanical, pendulum swing from "security" to "flexibility" but a core part of the state's strategy of development'. While precarious employment and working conditions are not a new development, Millar (2017) suggests that the question may be asked "*for whom* is precarity new?" Alberti et al. (2018, 3) note that "precarity is [the] consequence of an unequal distribution of protection within society, which leaves some groups more exposed to precariousness than others". However, they also caution against underestimating the "scope of change in the world of work and employment: it is not only 'the precariat' that has to deal with increasing precarity".

Indeed, one of the papers in this special issue (Stacey et al. 2021) deals with the working conditions of a profession that was once considered stable and secure. These are teachers who now work in far more precarious employment conditions, with a trend of hiring new teachers on short-term contracts, resulting in a two-tier system of educators (Plunkett and Dyson 2011).

The scope and visibility of precarious employment, often dubbed the 'gig economy' is a growing reality that educators must face both in their own work, and in the ways they prepare young people to move into their own futures.

Precarity, grounded in analyses of labour conditions and workers' experiences, has been taken up and applied to a range of unrelated areas. Indeed, Millar (2017) cautions that the concept of precarity is now so ubiquitous that it runs the risk of losing much of its meaning and analytical power. We have thus chosen in this editorial to delineate between precarity (a focus on working and labour conditions) and broader notions of precariousness - vulnerability, insecurity, and instability (Grenier et al. 2017; Millar 2017). Precarization has been described as '[penetrating] entire life-worlds of individuals and groups of people' (della Porta et al. 2015, 2).

This special issue goes to press at the end of 2021, after two years of global upheaval amid the COVID-19 pandemic. It is almost impossible to imagine not acknowledging COVID-19 in a reflection on these issues, though many of the papers were first written prior to the pandemic or in its early stages. The crisis has been described as accelerating social and political issues that already existed, as well as shining new light on existing inequities around the world (Gore et al. 2021; Reimer et al. 2021). Precariousness, as described above (vulnerability, insecurity, and instability) has been compounded by isolation, a collective and yet individualised grief, sense of fear, accompanied by an awareness that the future has irrevocably changed as a result of the pandemic and its consequences.

Crisis can result in rapid changes to political and social functions. For example, della Porta et al. (2015) remind us that structural transformations can sometimes be 'sudden and rapid', but that precarization has been a long and gradual process. It is yet to be seen what impact the COVID-19 pandemic will have long-term, but with over 5 million deaths worldwide (World Health Organization 2021), uneven effects on economies that disproportionately disadvantage developing nations (OECD 2021), and the decimation of higher education in some countries including Australia, where up to 40,000 university jobs are estimated to been lost (Blackmore 2020; Littleton and Stanford 2021), it can be assumed that the future we are preparing young people for will have changed in many fundamental ways.

The pathway for future generations will not be a straight line. della Porta et al. (2015, 3) describe the impossibility of providing useful advice to people experiencing precarity:

> one just cannot follow Descartes's advice that if one is lost in the forest, the best thing to do is simply to go straight ahead. Since precarization does not follow some uniform rational pattern but can be quite singular and even arbitrary – even if still structurally determined – the experiences of precariousness can also be complex, variable, fragmentary, and always quite particular.

Authors in this special issue were encouraged to take up theorisations and explorations of precarity that push our thinking further and enable new lines of inquiry into the discourses and practices shaping educational leadership in a time of precarity. The collection of papers in this special issue do just that. They explore precarious labour conditions, precariousness in policy and reform, and - importantly - they include a clear focus on the human experience at the centre of precariousness today.

The papers in the issue encompass three main themes:

1. supporting and preparing students for a precarious future,
2. an exploration of the labour conditions and experiences of education workers in precarious employment, and
3. broader notions of precariousness in relation to, or resulting from, education reforms.

## Supporting and Preparing Students for a Precarious Future

In *Theorising and preparing students for precarity: how can leaders and educators better prepare students to enter an increasingly insecure workforce?*, Lucas Walsh and Joanne Gleeson draw upon a study of 2500 Australian secondary school students to understand "the real and imagined characteristics of students as workers-in-the-making". Their analysis explores the intertwined nature of students' own identities with the broader context of labour and education. They reveal the importance of students seeing ways they might be able to plan for their futures so as to avoid leaving school feeling that these important decisions are out of their control. They raise implications for school leaders, teachers, and careers advisors to help prepare young people to navigate these futures.

Taking a different perspective towards preparing students for uncertain futures, Gail Crimmins, Briony Lipton, Joanna McIntyre, Margarietha de Villiers Scheepers and Peter English explore the ways universities prepare students for careers in creative industries, in their paper *Creative industries curriculum design for living and leading amid uncertainty*. Amid a policy environment which pushes universities to emphasise employability, they note that Creative Industries degrees have been criticised for "failing to deliver adequate employment prospects". Crimmins et al. argue that the employability discourse fails to recognise the reality of precarious employment within the creative sector, and they draw on Habermas to suggest that these discourses mean universities are less able to focus on serving the lifeworld of graduates. They present a case of curriculum design which can support students to "navigate multiple ideological geographies, facilitate employability, and contribute to civic society".

## Labour conditions and experiences of education workers in precarious employment and pressurised environments

Higher education has long been a site of increasing precarity in employment, exacerbated by the consequences of the COVID-19 pandemic for universities around the world (Blackmore 2020). Previous research has emphasised the need for non-tenured (sometimes described as sessional, casual, or adjunct) academics to be provided with resourcing and support to undertake research, even when their precarious employment contracts generally focus only on teaching (Heffernan 2018). Kathleen Smithers, Jess Harris, Mhorag Goff, Nerida Spina and Simon Bailey make an important contribution to our understanding of these inequities in higher education employment practices in *Ethical responsibilities of tenured academics supervising non-tenured researchers in times of neoliberalism and precarity*. Their work focuses on the tenured academics who employ and manage non-tenured researchers - with little to no training in how to effectively lead and develop others. They highlight the ethical responsibilities held by tenured academics to create a working environment that supports the development and wellbeing of non-tenured staff and push back against the idea that precarious academics - who make up a significant proportion of the academic workforce - are the 'other'.

Also exploring the experiences and implications for leaders of precarious employees are Meghan Stacey, Scott Fitzgerald, Rachel Wilson, Susan McGrath-Champ and Mihajla Gavin in *Teachers, fixed-term contracts and school leadership: toeing the line and jumping through hoops*. The authors explore the experiences of teachers in temporary employment. Their findings reveal that teachers in precarious employment feel like they need to 'prove themselves' to school leaders, which has implications for the ways they undertake their work, and their subsequent career progression. Stacey et al. highlight the implications of these findings for leaders, whom they caution should "ensure that they, or other permanent staff in the school, do not take advantage of this vulnerability through delegation of work, the 'dangling' of employment contracts or the local appointment of staff based on reasons other than merit". However, they recognise that leaders themselves are also under pressure, and suggest that meaningful change needs to come from above, particularly in relation to hiring and employment policies and practices.

Finally, Michael Jopling and Oliver Harness explore the precariousness felt by school leaders in England during the COVID-19 pandemic in their paper *Embracing vulnerability: How has Covid-19 affected the pressures school leaders in Northern England face and how they deal with them?* Jopling and Harness examined the experiences of leaders in North-East England during the pandemic, revealing the challenges they were experiencing, coupled with a lack of support for school leaders during a time when they were particularly vulnerable and under considerable pressure. They suggest that embracing vulnerability might be one way for leaders to cope with the precarity involved in their positions, and recognise when support is particularly needed.

## Education reform

The final theme addressed within this Special Issue is that of education reform and the precariousness of work, education practices, and policies as a result of ongoing reform.

In *Repositioned professionals and heterodox: a response to the precarity of reform in further education*, Lewis Entwistle draws upon Bourdieu's theories to understand the ways professionals working in further education in England are being continually reshaped by policies that emphasise marketisation and competition. He argues that "the field of Further Education is being restructured such that professionalism is hollowed out whilst accountability measures undermine leaders' authority and enable a low-trust culture". His paper provides some hope, with an exploration of alternative positions and ways of responding to the continuously changing field of education reform.

In *Necessary risk: addressing precarity by re-envisioning teaching and learning*, Jeanne M. Powers and Lok-Sze Wong explore the effects of long-term neoliberal education policy reforms in Arizona, USA which have left public schools and educators in positions of precariousness. Their paper also reflects the ongoing change caused by the COVID-19 pandemic, and explores a case study of one college of education's attempt to re-imagine "how students learn and how teachers work". They explore the affordances and challenges associated with these reforms amid the increased uncertainty and precariousness resulting from the COVID-19 pandemic.

The papers within this special issue are a collection of just some ways of thinking about these issues. We hope they are a starting point for further conversation and analysis. We invite research that builds upon these foundations to bring socially critical and historically informed analyses to issues of precarity, precariousness, and educational leadership. We thank the authors and reviewers for their energies and efforts throughout the past two years. Your work has ensured this special issue has come together to make a wide-ranging and important contribution to our understanding of these issues.

## ORCID

*Amanda Heffernan* ⓘ http://orcid.org/0000-0001-8306-5202
*Jane Wilkinson* ⓘ http://orcid.org/0000-0002-0727-0025

## References

Alberti, Gabriella, Ioulia Bessa, Kate Hardy, Vera Trappmann, and Charles Umney. 2018. "In, Against and Beyond Precarity: Work in Insecure Times." *Work, Employment and Society* 32 (3): 447–457.

Blackmore, J. 2020. "The Carelessness of Entrepreneurial Universities in a World Risk Society: A Feminist Reflection on the Impact of Covid-19 in Australia." *Higher Education Research & Development* 39 (7): 1332–1336. doi:10.1080/07294360.2020.1825348.

della Porta, Donatella, Sakari Hänninen, Martti Siisiäinen, and Tiina Silvasti. 2015. "The Precarization Effect." In *The New Social Division: Making and Unmaking Precariousness*, edited by Donatella della Porta, Sakari Hänninen, Martti Siisiäinen, and Tiina Silvasti, 1–24. London: Palgrave Macmillan.

Gore, Jennifer, Leanne Fray, Andrew Miller, Jess Harris, and Wendy Taggart. 2021. "The impact of COVID-19 on student learning in New South Wales primary schools: an empirical study." *The Australian Educational Researcher*, 1–33. Advance Online Article. doi:10.1007/s13384-021-00436-w.

Grenier, Amanda, Chris Phillipson, Debbie Laliberte Rudman, Stephanie Hatzifilalithis, Karen Kobayashi, and Patrik Marier. 2017. "Precarity in late life: Understanding new forms of risk and insecurity." *Journal of Aging Studies* 43: 9–14.

Heffernan, Troy. 2018. "Approaches to career development and support for sessional academics in higher education." *International Journal for Academic Development* 23 (4): 312–323.

Lee, Ching Kwan Lee, and Yelizavetta Kofman. 2012. "The Politics of Precarity: Views Beyond the United States." *Work and Occupations* 39 (4): 388–408. doi:10.1177/0730888412446710.

Littleton, Eliza, and Jim Stanford. 2021. *An Avoidable Catastrophe: Pandemic Job Losses in Higher Education and their Consequences.* Canberra: Centre for Future Work.

Millar, Kathleen M. 2017. "Toward a critical politics of precarity." *Sociology Compass* 11 (6): e12483. doi:10.1111/soc4.12483.

OECD. 2021. *OECD Economic Outlook, Interim Report September 2021: Keeping the Recovery on Track.* Paris: OECD Publishing. doi:10.1787/490d4832-en.

Plunkett, Margaret, and Michael Dyson. 2011. "Becoming a teacher and staying one: Examining the Complex Ecologies Associated with Educating and Retaining New Teachers in Rural Australia." *Australian Journal of Teacher Education* 36 (1): 32–47. doi:10.14221/ajte.2011v36n1.3.

Reimer, David, Emil Smith, Ida Gran Andersen, and Bent Sortkær. 2021. "What happens when schools shut down? Investigating inequality in students' reading behavior during Covid-19 in Denmark." *Research in Social Stratification and Mobility* 71: 100568.

Stacey, Meghan, Scott Fitzgerald, Rachel Wilson, Susan McGrath-Champ, and Mihajla Gavin. 2021. "Teachers, fixed-term contracts and school leadership: toeing the line and jumping through hoops." *Journal of Educational Administration and History* 54 (1). doi:10.1080/00220620.2021.1906633.

World Health Organization. 2021. *WHO Coronavirus (COVID-19) Dashboard.* https://covid19.who.int/.

# Theorising and preparing students for precarity: how can leaders and educators better prepare students to enter an increasingly insecure workforce?

Lucas Walsh ⓘ and Joanne Gleeson ⓘ

**ABSTRACT**
Workforce insecurity has significant implications for the role of school leaders and teachers preparing students for changing worlds of work. For educators to better prepare students to enter an increasingly casualised labour workforce, there first needs to be an acknowledgement of how students perceive themselves in relation to post-school life. Drawing on a study of approximately 2500 secondary school students in the Australian state of Victoria, the figure of homo promptus is presented as a figure of youth to understand the real and imagined characteristics of students as workers-in-the-making. Homo promptus is entrepreneurial and strategic, yet on 'standby' as short-termism problematises future planning. This figure is overlaid onto students' perceptions of their own career identity relative to post-school aspirations and transitions. The emergence of homo promptus and the broader labour and education landscapes from which this conceptualisation has been developed have implications for school leaders, teachers and school-based careers advisors.

## Introduction

Schooling in Australia focuses on supporting 'young people to realise their potential by providing skills they need to participate in the economy and in society' (Education Council 2019, 3). One of the implied promises of a better material life through education is its ability to pave pathways to meaningful work. But what if these pathways are eroding, or at the very least, shifting in seismic ways? How do school leaders respond to a world of work beyond the school gates that is fast becoming transformed by casualisation, insecurity and emergent constructs such as portfolio careers?

This paper aims to provide a way of thinking about youth subjectivities in relation to their working lives following school. Understanding what perceptions students have of themselves in relation to their post-school lives can inform how school leaders help them to better navigate transitions from school. The theoretical concept of homo promptus (Black and Walsh 2019) provides a lens through which such insights can be gained. Drawing on the findings from a large-scale study of approximately 2500 secondary school students in the southern Australian state of Victoria, the figure of homo promptus as entrepreneurial and strategic, yet on 'standby' as short-termism problematises future planning, is overlaid onto students' perceptions of their own career identity. The findings suggest that for some students, homo promptus is a conscious and lived identity. For others, homo promptus is a surreality, and either through denial or some form of false optimism, these students believe that their post-school transitions will be untainted, or at worst, lightly touched by precarity.

It is argued that school leaders, teachers and school-based careers advisors have obligations to not only acknowledge the emergence of homo promptus, as well as the broader labour and education landscapes from which this conceptualisation has been developed, but to ensure students and their parents are fully aware of and accept the ramifications of future precarity. From an historical perspective, this is currently not the case and is evidenced by out-dated approaches to careers education that over-emphasise student academic outcomes and post-school tertiary education pathways, and rely largely on traditional conceptualisations of careers as 'twentieth century, and even nineteenth century, occupations' (Mann et al. 2020, 12). Students' insights then are important to help inform effective careers education in the future (Jackson and Tomlinson 2020). They also make a significant contribution to the literature focussing on students' internalisations of current employment conditions, the value of higher education (HE), their own employability and career decision-making (Scurry and Blenkinsopp 2011).

## Employment and careers

Rapidly changing employment landscapes have impacted young Australians disproportionately (Walsh and Black 2018). The current COVID-19 pandemic has decimated employment opportunities for young people, many of whom were already engaged in precarious casual work. Teenagers and those aged 20–29 years have been most affected, and are now not only unemployed, but have little prospect of their jobs returning post-pandemic (Earl 2020; Jericho 2020). Even prior to this economic downturn, casual work was pervasive, with one in four Australian workers employed in a casual position, many of whom reported having no guaranteed hours, nor opportunities to convert their uncertain work contracts into more stable and fixed employment arrangements (Organization for Economic Co-operation and Development [OECD] 2019). Australia's rate of casualised work was and is one of the highest when compared with other OECD countries (OECD 2019). Leading into the pandemic, over half of all young Australian workers were engaged in casual employment, reporting lower working standards, remuneration, entitlements and job security than older employees (Dhillon and Cassidy 2018). One in three Australian youth suffered unemployment or under-employment (OECD 2019), with these rates likely to increase and be the worst experienced in decades (Wright 2020).

Prior to the severe economic impacts of COVID-19, demographic shifts, labour market regulations, macroeconomic fluctuations and technological changes have been transforming labour markets globally over recent decades. In the 1980s and 1990s, for example, worsening global economic conditions resulted in significant organisational structure and workforce changes that shifted traditional career profiles to ones that were uncertain and insecure (Clarke 2013). This led to questions at the time as to whether a single, linear, long-term, upwardly-trajectorial career had ceased to exist (Wyn et al. 2020). Fast-forward to 2020, and increasingly fluid and precarious global employment markets continue to reshape work profiles, with expansions in the number of people engaged in transient, insecure, under-employed and short-term work arrangements (International Labour Organization [ILO] 2020). Career imaginaries have been forced then to move away from occupations or a sequence of organisational roles and statuses to more 'flexible' notions (Clarke 2013; Tomlinson et al. 2018) that are hallmarked by a person's inter-organisational mobility, flexibility, temporary and multiple employer relationships, and individual accountability for adaptable career management and ambition. Terms such as 'boundaryless', 'protean', 'portfolio', and 'kaleidoscope' have entered career lexicons in attempts to capture more effectively what a person's career looks like relevant to current employment landscapes (Gubler, Arnold, and Coombs 2014).

Of most significance to young people in this context has been the break-down of the long-held assumption that HE qualifications will lead to desirable and secure work (Chesters and Wyn 2019; Wyn et al. 2020). Recent data has suggested that even medium to highly educated young people have experienced increases in their probabilities of low-paid employment in Australia in the last decade (OECD 2019). Noting the trends in changing labour markets and traditional job profiles, not only are there fewer full-time permanent jobs available for the increasing numbers of highly qualified job seekers (Chesters and Wyn 2019), but graduates have reported experiencing labour market mismatches despite their qualifications, including skill underutilisation and poor job quality and choices (Li, Harris, and Sloane 2018). This is creating concern for young people (Wyn et al. 2020), which will only be exacerbated in post-pandemic times. They not only feel pressured to seek credentials and experiences to improve their employability in competitive employment markets (Black and Walsh 2019; Oinonen 2018), but feel disillusioned and betrayed by the trap in which they find themselves (Chesters and Wyn 2019). While higher qualifications remain crucial to securing desirable work, the sum of these trends and evidence has profound implications for how careers education needs to be conceived and implemented in Australian schools.

## Careers education in Australian schools

Careers education in Australian schools though appears out-of-date in its approaches to helping students understand and prepare for post-school transitions. Academic outcomes and tertiary destinations post-school are overly-emphasised as measures of students' success (O'Connell, Milligan, and Bentley 2019), with students then funnelled to tertiary education over and above other post-school pathways (Torii and O'Connell 2017). These practices are concerning, with Australian studies showing that many students enrol at university without knowing why they are doing so, what courses would be best for them, or what employment could result from their qualifications (Baik, Naylor, and Arkoudis 2015; Parks et al. 2017). In a vast number of cases, students enrol with no intentions of ever completing, drop out and in hindsight, believe they should not have started in the first place (Norton, Cherastidtham, and Mackey 2018).

Concerns have also been raised regarding the stratification of information and advice provided to students based on teachers' and advisors' preconceptions of who apparently is better suited to tertiary education pathways and who is not (Gore et al. 2017; Graham, Van Bergen, and Sweller 2015). Advice provided to students regarding alternative post-school pathways has been found at times to be untrustworthy, uneven or based on inadequate knowledge (Bisson and Stubley 2017; Wyman et al. 2017). Careers education also appears caught in 'old paradigms' of occupations and work that promulgate young people's expectations of a long-term, single professional career as the ideal (Shergold et al. 2020, 57). Students hear messages then that going to university post-school will result in a 'good' career, whilst not going to university will result in a 'bad' one (Billett, Choy, and Hodge 2020; Torii and O'Connell 2017). Despite ever-changing global employment landscapes, these preconceptions, alongside concomitant messages from parents, are so strong that many young Australians, irrespective of gender or socio-economic status, conjure preferred career trajectories that are professional, status-oriented and secure (Baxter 2017; Roy, Barker, and Stafford 2019).

When many of these aspirations go unrealised (Billett, Choy, and Hodge 2020; Mann et al. 2020), what results then is a career identity crisis for young people. Contradictions between cultural messages of career success, biased or ill-informed advice, and post-school employment market realities mean that students hear and internalise one thing, but potentially experience another (Verhoeven, Poorthuis, and Volman 2019). Recent research has shown that whilst young Australians accept the probability of precarious employment during their studies, they expect to not only secure full-time, permanent employment post-education (Cuervo and Wyn 2016), but that it will be 'career-related' (Co-op 2015). And whilst young workers in Australia and other countries may be anxious about their longer-range career prospects, this does not mean that they still don't aspire to or want stable, long-term careers that are fashioned along traditional lines (Black and Walsh 2019; Pennington and Stanford 2019).

If schools and institutions are to assist students prepare for challenging employment landscapes more effectively, then it is argued that students' employability needs to be framed around their own career identity development (Nghia et al. 2020). Students need to 'internalise the dearth of traditional careers' (Jackson and Tomlinson 2020, 437) and be supported to connect their own career capital resources – functional, human, social and cultural capitals – with knowledgeable but more importantly, realistic perceptions of worlds-of-work. The more students can do this, then the more they will be able to imagine and make sense of themselves in future work roles and navigate post-school transitions accordingly (Skorikov and Vondracek 2011).

## Method

The survey was one instrument as part of a wider study to validate a measure of adolescent career identity. Following ethics approval from the Victorian Department of Education, the relevant Catholic Diocese and the university in which both authors are based, the survey was administered in 2018 to Years 10–12 students (the final years of compulsory schooling in Australia) in five participating schools as a university-licensed Qualtrics-based online survey. Following consent from each school principal, student assent to participate was implied if the survey was completed.

The survey comprised three sections, the first of which focused on personal information, and the second on information regarding future study and career intentions. The final section comprised 50 items to be rated according to a 5-point Likert-type rating scale: *Strongly Disagree – Strongly Agree*. The statements focused on understanding respondents' perspectives of their own career identity including: human, social and cultural capitals relative to their future study-career aspirations; career planning abilities; perceived employability and skills such as flexibility and resilience; connections with current employment conditions; and functional capital including self-awareness and self-esteem. 32 statements were worded positively, with 18 worded negatively, responses from which would be reverse coded. The survey took 30–40 minutes and was completed by 2895 students, with 2473 valid responses. Respondent details are included in the Supplementary Material.

The conceptual lens through which data has been analysed is the figure of homo promptus. This figure is derived from Cicero

> to describe a person who is ready to do whatever is needed in any circumstance ... homo promptus is: entrepreneurial and strategic; expected to constantly plan for the future while living life in the short-term; not tethered to a single place; permanently in 'situational' mode; and lives in waithood. (Walsh and Black 2020, 3–4)

Formulated to better understand the attitudes of a small cohort of university students in Australia, France and Great Britain, homo promptus is a conceptual figure of selfhood that helps to describe the types of emergent sociological conditions of young people as workers or workers-in-the-making.

Threadgold (2020) identifies a plethora of figures of youth that have been conceived, including, for example, young people as figures of moral panic and revolution, representing risks to both themselves and others, as 'consumer dupes', where youth, as an image, is invoked as an 'enjoyable, carefree, state of leisure', as well as morally corrupt (Threadgold 2020, 691–696). Homo promptus seeks to elide the normative and sometimes affective associations of these images. In part, homo promptus is derived from trajectory of thought about cultivation of the entrepreneurial self which leads from Rose (1996) through Peters (2001) to Kelly (2016). It also seeks to incorporate other recent writings about youth subjectivities seeking to understand both the 'positive' and 'negative' aspects of youth transitions (Honwana 2014). A novel aspect of our approach is to connect homo promptus to the testimonies of young people in relation to career identity. Drawing from the 'meaningful orientations' of respondents, homo promptus is presented as one way of understanding and characterising the contemporary experiences of young people in relation to employment, but it is by no means a fully representative one due to the continued diversity of young people's experiences and perceptions, as captured in this study.

## Findings

The findings are firstly unpacked in relation to how they reflect the figure of homo promptus, but it is important to highlight that not all attitudes neatly fit into the frame of this figure. That the perspectives of young people defy neat categorisation is a longstanding finding in youth studies (Black and Walsh 2019). It is also important to note that the student sample is diverse, with regards to gender, socioeconomic status [SES] and geography in particular. The data does show differences across these demographics, but unpacking these requires a deeper analysis than is afforded here, and will form the basis of a future paper.

Overall, most respondents believed that they would be employable in the future (79.1 percent), but significant nuances emerge in their imagined future pathways. Three aspects of this are evident in the findings: a worry about the competitive nature of the job market; a feeling of need to be flexible and adaptable as a basis for preparing for working life; and a lack of readiness about future careers.

## Entrepreneurial and strategic: 'I am studying and taking on different activities so that I have the best skill set for my preferred career'

Homo promptus is entrepreneurial. In 2020, policy and employment market realities necessitate students' employability narratives to be ones of 'self-enterprise', where they consciously and constantly better themselves and relate 'to others as competitors and [their] own being as a form of human capital' (McNay 2009, 63). Many of the respondents seemed to value the development of skills and experiences to add to their perceived employability through a variety of activities. In response to the proposition that 'I am studying and taking on different activities so that I have the best skill set for my preferred career', 55 percent agreed. Further, more than half (54.4 percent) agreed that they were 'gaining the work experience, skills and education that will give me the best chances of attaining my preferred career'. A majority (75 percent) agreed that 'My career choices suit my strengths and interests', with a similar proportion agreeing that 'My future career will allow me to apply all the skills I am best at' (76.1 percent).

Students' orientation towards employability echoes previous research showing a shift in the way that young people think about careers and the support that they require. Australian students are very concerned that they don't possess the relevant experience and skills to gain the careers that they want in current employment contexts (Marks 2017). As a result, like students in many other countries, they are taking action to gain skills and knowledge through activities external to their education including participation in extra-curricular activities, work experience and volunteering (Jackson and Tomlinson 2020). Students' call-to-action for schools and employers is that they want better access to a broader range of experiences and skill development, as well as connections with industry (Bisson and Stubley 2017; Down, Smyth, and Robinson 2018). Most importantly, through comprehensive and objective careers education (Torii and O'Connell 2017), they want help crafting their own employability and 'career narratives' that integrate their strengths, interests and experiences relevant to future work roles (Stokes, Wierenga, and Wyn 2003, 81–82).

Of striking interest though was the finding that nearly 36 percent of all respondents agreed with the proposition that 'I feel like I am studying and taking on activities without any sense of purpose or career direction' (totalling 67.4 percent when neutral/unsure responses were combined). This may suggest a type of 'follow the leader' behaviour or an undertone of concern that if activities are not undertaken, then students may feel 'left behind'. As an adjunct to this concern is the finding that nearly half of all respondents (totalling 72.8 percent when neutral/unsure responses were combined) feel that they have 'missed opportunities to maximise their potential to achieve their future careers', with lower SES students feeling most vulnerable. Whilst focused on the higher education sector, research suggests that students' awareness and concern of competition from others motivates their involvement, or desires to be involved, in work experience and extra-curricular activities (e.g. Tomlinson 2008). Students are also 'heavily influenced by a desire to conform to social norms and the normative behaviour of their peers' (Greenbank 2015, 194), which may explain their uptake of and attraction to extra-curricular activities potentially for little obvious reason. The findings may also suggest that students have an intuition that these types of 'employability' behaviours are necessary, but with no career direction. Whilst students acknowledge the need to differentiate themselves from others and build their employability, they may not be able to connect extra-curricular activities or work experiences with their career aspirations or plans because these are ill-defined (Thompson et al. 2013), or because 'employment' or 'starting their career' are too far into the future (Tymon 2013). Students may also be undertaking extra-curricular activities or work simply for interest or enjoyment and may not make career-related connections as a result (Denault et al. 2019). The findings may even suggest a disconnect between their understandings of employment market realities and how to respond (Jackson and Tomlinson 2020).

## Competition, uncertainty and contingency: 'I am flexible and can deal with different challenges to achieve my career goals'

Homo promptus also embraces uncertainty and contingency, and understands the need to be 'constantly "on the move" and seeking to position themselves competitively' (Black and Walsh 2019, 96). As a corollary of pursuing activities seen to be strategically beneficial to imagined careers, current economic and employment conditions necessitate students to be agile, flexible, resilient and adaptive to change (Duarte, da Silva, and Paixão 2017; Smith 2018). The vast majority of respondents agreed that 'I am flexible and can deal with different challenges to achieve my career goals' (76.9 percent). Most also accepted that their career path 'will not always be clear and known' to them (64.4 percent). And if their preferred career choice was not possible, they felt able 'to make different career decisions and move forward' (52.3 percent; 83.8 percent when neutral/unsure responses were combined). Further, just over half believed that their career 'will be made up of different jobs and roles' (56.6 percent agreed; 90.2 percent when neutral/unsure responses were combined). Mindful of employment competition, most claimed that they had 'thought about future jobs and employment potential when making career decisions' (66.4 percent agreed).

A thread running throughout responses though was a concern, if not anxiety, about future opportunities. Just over a third (33.9 percent) agreed that 'I worry that my studies will not lead to a "real" career', with over half (52.7 percent) worried 'what will happen if I can't meet my career goals exactly as I have planned'. These concerns about career certainty, control and security were skewed heavily towards female respondents from all schools, irrespective of geography or SES. Many respondents (43.1 percent) were worried 'that there are too many people going for the same career and jobs that I want' (72.4 percent when neutral/unsure responses were combined), with a notable proportion worried 'that there are not many jobs in my preferred career' (38.9 percent agreed; 69.7 percent when neutral/unsure responses were combined). Pressure to compete for employment with others was a concern for lower SES respondents especially when compared with high SES counterparts. Overall, similar feelings of anxiety about future employment opportunities are consistent with other Australian data (e.g. Wyn et al. 2020), and are only likely to worsen post-pandemic (Headspace 2020).

## Mutable futures: 'My career path will not always be clear and known'

There is also an aspect of homo promptus which sees the future as 'mainly unknowable' (Black and Walsh 2019, 98). Studies show that young Australians are inhabiting a 'continuous present' (Bone 2019), whereby future uncertainty is normalised and abilities to plan are curtailed (Cuervo and Chesters 2019). How well individuals cope with this 'unknowing' depends on many things including, amongst others, SES background, support networks, personal dispositions, skills, knowledge and resources. At face value, respondents reflected both an expectation of and confidence in change, with most acknowledging that their career choices and plans would shift over time (59.5 percent). They indicated a sense of agency, feeling that when faced with different career options, they could 'pick the one that best suits me' (66.3 percent). Most also accepted that their career path 'will not always be clear and known' to them (64.4 percent), with just over half feeling 'able to make different career decisions and move forward' if a preferred career choice was not possible (52.3 percent agreed; 83.8 percent when neutral or unsure responses were combined). These findings potentially show students as having 'career malleability', that is, an acceptance that career futures cannot be predicted coupled with a confidence that if circumstances change, they can 'rewrite or refashion their career narrative' (Skrbiš and Laughland-Booÿ 2019, 202). Careers in this light are viewed as flexible, with unknown futures not something to fear or uncertainty not a negative emotion that needs to be reduced (Zinn 2006).

Yet, counter to this are young people who have or show career insecurity, hallmarked by an unknown career future that erodes present confidence and abilities to plan or set goals (Skrbiš and Laughland-Booÿ 2019). Just over 40 percent of respondents did not know what careers best suited them, with significantly more feeling unprepared, unclear and purposeless. This, in turn, was causing feelings of stress and anxiety. For example, many respondents often felt down or worried about selecting a career (40.6 percent agreed; 70.9 percent when neutral/unsure responses were combined), or that their 'career path will not always be clear and known' to them (46.7 percent agreed; 78.3 percent when neutral/unsure responses were combined). Further, over half felt 'stress or pressure to select the "right" career' (55.4 percent; 80 percent when neutral/ unsure responses were combined), with a high proportion concerned that they would not be employable post-school (37.2 percent agreed; 65.7 percent when neutral/unsure responses were combined). Female respondents, particularly those from high SES backgrounds, felt most insecure and pressured about career decisions and future pathways.

## Discussion

The figure of homo promptus helps to outline the shape of contemporary career identity as a sociological phenomenon. Our analysis reveals that at face value, students appear to expect – if not embrace – the precarious futures that lie ahead of them, expressing confidence in their entrepreneurialism, strategic thinking and agile decision-making and planning abilities to pivot when needed. Cognisant of current employment conditions, they appear savvy investors and believers in their own employability. Yet, this may all be bluff. Strong tones of concern and uncertainty are woven through students' responses, revealing that they may not actually be able to reconcile career precarity with their own aspirations or future expectations. These dichotomies are telling. Homo promptus might therefore loom large for some students, casting shadows because of his reality or students' own unpreparedness and lack of abilities to internalise his persona. For others, the spectre of homo promptus is unrelated to their aspirations and confidence in themselves and not necessary to internalise at all. And somewhere in the middle, students warily perceive homo promptus, reflexively describing mantras of flexibility and individuality expected of them, but potentially not really believing them, or if they do, not knowing or accepting fully the reality of what homo promptus has in store for them.

Several insights gained from our analysis are important to be able to position careers education differently for young Australians. First, similar to previous research, young people prepare for future employment landscapes and craft their career-selves in complex and often contradictory ways that mix confidence and anxiety, optimism and pessimism (Woodman 2011). Untangling the 'real' perceptions that are influencing individual students' own career identity is a critical task for school leaders. It is therefore not acceptable to continue making assumptions about or ignoring the realities of different occupations, career pathways and employment markets, applying these preconceptions to students as a 'job-lot' and then expecting them, individually, to be able to navigate post-school transitions effectively. For example, drawing on data from the research study featured in this paper, when asked about the appropriateness of proposed career identity survey questions intended for administration to students, one school leader stated:

> Students in our school will not believe that labour markets or future jobs are relevant to them … Information or knowledge of current labour markets is not something we believe they need to think about or incorporate into career decision-making whilst still at school. (Senior school leader; all female, P-12 independent, high socio-economic school)

That students are placed in positions where they hear and internalise irresponsible messages such as this is problematic. School leaders should be cognisant that the basis of career identity is changing, but more-over, that education should focus on more than just preparing young people to tread water in the choppy seas ahead, but to navigate and reimagine for themselves the very basis of how work relates to their individual identities. Effective careers education also needs to be nuanced to the contexts in which students live, accounting for factors such as their SES and gender identification for example. Careers education needs to be deeply attuned to where young people are in their present lives and their imagined futures.

Further, short-termism, flexibility and fluidity, whether acceptable or believable or not, are normalised within current employment market realities. Rosa (2015) argues that when futures are 'unforeseeable and uncontrollable, "situational" or present-oriented patterns of identity dominate' (146). Yet, coping with and planning around the unknown and embracing career malleability goes against the very notions of forward planning and aspiring to long-term career trajectories that hallmark current school-based careers education (Adam 2010). Helping students balance and reconcile situational decision-making and contingent career planning such that they don't feel that their futures are happening *to them* rather than be crafted *by them* are challenges that need to be confronted by school leaders. If students leave school feeling not only under-prepared but out of control, then their 'present' uncertainty and anxiety is at risk of being drawn-out (Bone 2019).

## Conclusion

Homo promptus is presented as a figure of youth to understand the real and imagined characteristics of students as workers-in-the-making. While experiences of homo promptus are varied, this figure can shed light on how educators can critically engage with the preparation of students for employment during a time of precarity. Following this, students themselves are ideally able to critically engage with their lives post-school and, where necessary, imagine better alternatives. School leaders and their communities may then be better placed to work with young people to shape their post-school lives, rather than be subject to the imagined and real demands of flexibility, contingency and uncertainty. To this last aspect, further research is needed into the extent to which the uncertainty that underpins much of the discourse around contemporary work is potentially manufactured by employers (e.g. by proponents of the so-called 'gig economy') to deliberately harness workforce docility and drive down wages and entitlements. Furthermore, navigating the contemporary workforce requires more than the skills to navigate uncertainty: it requires a deep knowledge of what has transpired before combined with the critical faculty to imagine lives beyond homo promptus.

## Disclosure statement

No potential conflict of interest was reported by the author(s).

## ORCID

*Lucas Walsh* ⓘ http://orcid.org/0000-0002-7224-2135
*Joanne Gleeson* ⓘ http://orcid.org/0000-0002-0977-9482

## References

Adam, B. 2010. "History of the Future: Paradoxes and Challenges." *Rethinking History* 14 (3): 361–378.

Baik, C., R. Naylor, and S. Arkoudis. 2015. *The First-Year Experience in Australian Universities: Findings from Two Decades, 1994–2014.* Carlton: Melbourne Centre for the Study of Higher Education, University of Melbourne. https://melbourne-cshe.unimelb.edu.au/__data/assets/pdf_file/0016/1513123/FYE-2014-FULL-report-FINAL-web.pdf.

Baxter, J. 2017. "The Career Aspirations of Young Adolescent Boys and Girls." In *Growing Up in Australia: LSAC Annual Statistical Report 2016*, edited by K. Day, 11 –34. Sydney: Australian Institute of Family Studies.

Billett, S., S. Choy, and S. Hodge. 2020. "Enhancing the Standing of Vocational Education and the Occupations It Serves: Australia." *Journal of Vocational Education & Training* 72 (2): 270–296.

Bisson, R., and W. Stubley. 2017. *After the ATAR: Understanding How Gen Z Transition into Further Education and Employment*. Sydney: Year13. https://www.voced.edu.au/content/ngv%3A77228.

Black, R., and L. Walsh. 2019. *Imagining Youth Futures: University Students in Post-Truth Times*. New York: Springer.

Bone, K. D. 2019. "I Don't Want to Be a Vagrant for the Rest of My Life: Young Peoples' Experiences of Precarious Work as a 'Continuous Present'." *Journal of Youth Studies* 22 (9): 1218–1237.

Chesters, J., and J. Wyn. 2019. "Chasing Rainbows: How Many Educational Qualifications Do Young People Need to Acquire Meaningful, Ongoing Work?" *Journal of Sociology* 55 (4): 670–688.

Clarke, M. 2013. "The Organizational Career: Not Dead but in Need of Redefinition." *The International Journal of Human Resource Management* 24 (4): 684–703.

Co-op. 2015. *2015 Future Leaders Index: Career and Employment. White Paper 3*. Sydney: BDO. https://www.bdo.com.au/en-au/insights/publications/future-leaders-index/future-leaders-index-part-3.

Cuervo, H., and J. Chesters. 2019. "The [Im]possibility of Planning a Future: How Prolonged Precarious Employment During Transitions Affects the Lives of Young Australians." *Labour & Industry: A Journal of the Social and Economic Relations of Work* 29 (4): 295–312.

Cuervo, H., and J. Wyn. 2016. "An Unspoken Crisis: The 'Scarring Effects' of the Complex Nexus Between Education and Work on Two Generations of Young Australians." *International Journal of Lifelong Education* 35 (2): 122–135.

Denault, A.-S., C. F. Ratelle, S. Duchesne, and F. Guay. 2019. "Extracurricular Activities and Career Indecision: A Look at the Mediating Role of Vocational Exploration." *Journal of Vocational Behavior* 110: 43–53.

Dhillon, Z., and N. Cassidy. 2018. *Labour Market Outcomes for Younger People: Bulletin, June 2018*. Sydney: Reserve Bank of Australia. https://www.rba.gov.au/publications/bulletin/2018/jun/labour-market-outcomes-for-younger-people.html.

Down, B., J. Smyth, and J. Robinson. 2018. *Rethinking School-to-Work Transitions in Australia: Young People Have Something to Say*. New York: Springer.

Duarte, M. E., J. T. da Silva, and M. P. Paixão. 2017. "Career Adaptability, Employability, and Career Resilience in Managing Transitions." In *Pscyhology of Career Adaptability, Employability and Resilience*, edited by K. Maree, 241–261. New York: Springer.

Earl, R. 2020. "Youth Unemployment Crisis Is Unfolding Before Our Eyes." *The Canberra Times*, June 10. https://www.canberratimes.com.au/story/6775436/youth-unemployment-crisis-is-unfolding-before-our-eyes/#gsc.tab=0.

Education Council. 2019. *The Alice Springs (Mparntwe) Education Declaration*. Canberra: Education Council. https://docs.education.gov.au/documents/alice-springs-mparntwe-education-declaration.

Gore, J., K. Holmes, M. Smith, L. Fray, P. McElduff, N. Weaver, and C. Wallington. 2017. "Unpacking the Career Aspirations of Australian School Students: Towards an Evidence Base for University Equity Initiatives in Schools." *Higher Education Research & Development* 36 (7): 1383–1400.

Graham, L. J., P. Van Bergen, and N. Sweller. 2015. "'To Educate You to be Smart': Disaffected Students and the Purpose of School in the (Not So Clever) 'Lucky Country'." *Journal of Education Policy* 30 (2): 237–257.

Greenbank, P. 2015. "Still Focusing on the 'Essential 2:1': Exploring Student Attitudes to Extra-curricular Activities." *Education + Training* 57 (2): 184–203.

Gubler, M., J. Arnold, and C. Coombs. 2014. "Reassessing the Protean Career Concept: Empirical Findings, Conceptual Components, and Measurement." *Journal of Organizational Behavior* 35: 23–40.

Headspace. 2020. "New Research: Young Australians Fearful and Uncertain for their Future." *National Youth Mental Health Foundation*, June 19. https://headspace.org.au/headspace-centres/mount-druitt/new-research-young-australians-fearful-and-uncertain-for-their-future/.

Honwana, A. 2014. "Waithood: Youth Transitions and Social Change." In *Development and Equity: An Interdisciplinary Exploration by Ten Scholars from Africa, Asia and Latin America*, edited by D. Foeken, T. Dietz, L. Haan, and L. Johnson, 28–40. Leiden: Brill Online.

International Labour Organization. 2020. *Non-Standard Forms of Employment*. Geneva: ILO. https://www.ilo.org/global/topics/non-standard-employment/lang--en/index.htm.

Jackson, D., and M. Tomlinson. 2020. "Investigating the Relationship Between Career Planning, Proactivity and Employability Perceptions Among Higher Education Students in Uncertain Labour Market Conditions." *Higher Education* 80: 435–455.

Jericho, G. 2020. "The Unemployment Rate Gets the Headlines but It's Underemployment We Should Look Out For." *The Guardian*, May 11. https://www.theguardian.com/business/grogonomics/2020/may/19/the-unemployment-rate-gets-the-headlines-but-its-underemployment-we-should-look-out-for.

Kelly, P. 2016. *The Self as Enterprise: Foucault and the Spirit of 21st Century Capitalism*. Surrey: Gower.

Li, I. W., M. N. Harris, and P. J. Sloane. 2018. "Vertical, Horizontal and Residual Skills Mismatch in the Australian Graduate Labour Market." *Economic Record* 94 (306): 301–315.

Mann, A., V. Denis, A. Schleicher, H. Ekhtiari, T. Forsyth, E. Liu, and N. Chambers. 2020. *Dream Jobs? Teenagers' Career Aspirations and the Future of Work*. Paris: OECD. https://www.oecd.org/berlin/publikationen/Dream-Jobs.pdf.

Marks, G. N. 2017. "University and Vocational Education, and Youth Labour Market Outcomes in Australia." *Journal of Education and Work* 30 (8): 868–880.

McNay, L. 2009. "Self as Enterprise: Dilemmas of Control and Resistance in Foucault's 'The Birth of Biopolitics'." *Theory, Culture and Society* 26 (6): 55–77.

Nghia, T. L. H., T. Pham, M. Tomlinson, K. Medica, and C. D. Thompson. 2020. "The Way Ahead for the Employability Agenda in Higher Education." In *Developing and Utilizing Employability Capitals: Graduates' Strategies across Labour Markets*, edited by T. L. H. Nghia, T. Pham, M. Tomlinson, K. Medica, and C. D. Thompson, 256–276. Abingdon: Routledge.

Norton, A., I. Cherastidtham, and W. Mackey. 2018. *Dropping Out: The Benefits and Costs of Trying University*. Carlton: Grattan Institute. https://grattan.edu.au/report/dropping-out/.

O'Connell, M., S. Milligan, and T. Bentley. 2019. *Beyond ATAR: A Proposal for Change*. Melbourne: Koshland Innovation Fund. https://www.all-learning.org.au/programs/beyond-atar-proposal-change.

Oinonen, E. 2018. "Under Pressure to Become: From a Student to Entrepreneurial Self." *Journal of Youth Studies* 21 (10): 1344–1360.

Organization for Economic Co-operation and Development. 2019. *The Future of Work: How Does AUSTRALIA Compare? OECD Employment Outlook 2019*. Paris: OECD.

Parks, A., J. E. Mills, D. Weber, M. Westwell, and K. Barovich. 2017. "What Should I Study? An Exploration of the Study Choices of Year 12 Students." Paper Presented at 2017 CDAA National Conference. http://whatshouldistudy.com.au/wp-content/uploads/2016/04/What-Should-I-Study-2017-CDAA-Conference-Paper-Parks-Mills-Weber-Westwell-and-Barovich.pdf.

Pennington, A., and J. Stanford. 2019. *The Future of Work for Australian Graduates: The Changing Landscape of University-Employment Transitions in Australia*. Canberra: Centre for Future Work, Australia Institute. https://www.futurework.org.au/the_future_of_work_for_australian_graduates.

Peters, M. 2001. "Education, Enterprise Culture and the Entrepreneurial Self: A Foucauldian Perspective." *Journal of Educational Enquiry* 2 (2): 58–71.

Rosa, H. 2015. *Social Acceleration: A New Theory of Modernity*. New York: Colombia University Press.

Rose, N. 1996. *Inventing Our Selves: Psychology, Power, and Personhood*. New York: Cambridge University Press.

Roy, A., B. Barker, and N. Stafford. 2019. *Please Just Say You are Proud of Me: Perspectives of Young People on Parent Engagement and Doing Well at School*. Canberra: ARACY. https://www.aracy.org.au/publications-resources/area?command=record&id=292.

Scurry, T., and J. Blenkinsopp. 2011. "Under-Employment Among Recent Graduates: A Review of the Literature." *Personnel Review* 40 (5): 643–659.

Shergold, P., T. Calma, S. Russo, P. Walton, J. Westacott, D. Zoellner, and P. O'Reilly. 2020. *Looking to the Future: Report of the Review of Senior Secondary Pathways into Work, Further Education and Training.* Canberra: Education Council. https://www.pathwaysreview.edu.au/.

Skorikov, V. B., and F. W. Vondracek. 2011. "Occupational Identity." In *Handbook of Identity Theory and Research*, edited by S. J. Schwartz, K. Luyckx, and V. L. Vignoles, 693–714. New York: Springer.

Skrbiš, Z., and J. Laughland-Booÿ. 2019. "Technology, Change, and Uncertainty: Maintaining Career Confidence in the Early 21st Century." *New Technology, Work and Employment* 34 (3): 191–207.

Smith, M. A. 2018. *Why Career Advice Sucks™: Join Generation Flux and Build an Agile, Flexible, Adaptable, and Resilient Career.* De Pere: Kompelling Publishing.

Stokes, H., A. Wierenga, and J. Wyn. 2003. *Young People's Perceptions of Career Education, VET, Enterprise Education and Part-Time Work.* Canberra: Enterprise and Career Education Foundation, DEST. http://web.education.unimelb.edu.au/yrc/linked_documents/RR24.pdf.

Thompson, L. J., G. Clark, M. Walker, and J. D. Whyatt. 2013. "'It's Just Like an Extra String to Your Bow': Exploring Higher Education Students' Perceptions and Experiences of Extracurricular Activity and Employability." *Active Learning in Higher Education* 14 (2): 135–147.

Threadgold, S. 2020. "Figures of Youth: On the Very Object of Youth Studies." *Journal of Youth Studies* 23 (6): 686–701.

Tomlinson, M. 2008. "The Degree Is Not Enough: Students' Perceptions of the Role of Higher Education Credentials for Graduate Work and Employability." *British Journal of Sociology of Education* 29 (1): 49–61.

Tomlinson, J., M. Baird, P. Berg, and R. Cooper. 2018. "Flexible Careers Across the Life Course: Advancing Theory and Practice." *Human Relations* 71 (1): 4–22.

Torii, K., and M. O'Connell. 2017. *Preparing Young People for the Future of Work: Mitchell Institute Report No. 01/2017.* Melbourne: Mitchell Institute. https://www.vu.edu.au/mitchell-institute/schooling/preparing-young-people-for-the-future-of-work.

Tymon, A. 2013. "The Student Perspective on Employability." *Studies in Higher Education* 38 (6): 841–856.

Verhoeven, M., A. M. G. Poorthuis, and M. Volman. 2019. "The Role of School in Adolescents' Identity Development: A Literature Review." *Educational Psychology Review* 31: 35–63.

Walsh, L., and R. Black. 2018. *Rethinking Youth Citizenship After the Age of Entitlement.* London: Bloomsbury Academic Publishing.

Walsh, L., and R. Black. 2020. "'Flexible Ongoing': The Young University Student as Homo Promptus." *Journal of Youth Studies*, doi:10.1080/13676261.2020.1742302.

Woodman, D. 2011. "Young People and the Future: Multiple Temporal Orientations Shaped in Interaction with Significant Others." *Young* 19 (2): 111–128.

Wright, S. 2020. "World Will Suffer a Recession: S&P." *The Age*, March 18. https://www.theage.com.au/politics/federal/world-will-suffer-a-recession-s-and-p-20200318-p54b97.html.

Wyman, N., M. McCrindle, S. Whatmore, J. Gedge, and T. Edwards. 2017. *Perceptions Are Not Reality: Myths, Realities and the Critical Role of Vocational Education & Training in Australia.* Abbotsford: Skilling Australia Foundation. https://saf.org.au/vet-sector-key-to-future-proofing-economy/.

Wyn, J., H. Cahill, D. Woodman, H. Cuervo, C. Leccardi, and J. Chesters. 2020. *Youth and the New Adulthood: Generations of Change.* New York: Springer.

Zinn, J. O. 2006. "Recent Developments in Sociology of Risk and Uncertainty." *Historical Social Research* 31 (2): 275–286.

# Creative industries curriculum design for living and leading amid uncertainty

Gail Crimmins ⓘ, Briony Lipton, Joanna McIntyre ⓘ, Margarietha de Villiers Scheepers ⓘ and Peter English

**ABSTRACT**
Government policies are forcing universities to narrowly emphasise employability, which does not bode well for the Creative Industries (CI). Despite being one of the fastest-growing and diverse employment sectors, CI degrees have been criticised for failing to deliver adequate employment prospects. The employability focus, which serves 'the [economic] system' [Habermas, Jürgen. 1987. *The Theory of Communicative Action. Volume 2 Lifeworld and Ssystem: The Ccritique of Functionalist reason*, Translated by T McCarthy. Cambridge: Polity Press], ignores both the employment precarity in the sector and diminishes universities' capacity to serve the lifeworld (Harbernas) to facilitate graduate citizenship. Dichotomising employability and citizenship fail to consider the supercomplexity of the twenty-first Century [Barnett, Ronald. 2000a. *Realizing the University in an Age of Supercomplexity*. Buckingham: Open University Press], constituted by the co-existence of a multiplicity of epistemological frameworks. In this paper, we draw on supercomplexity and the concept of the system and lifeworld to investigate how to develop CI curricula that foster employability and citizenship. Using an illustrative case, we demonstrate how CI curricula can be designed to support students to navigate multiple ideological geographies, facilitate employability, and contribute to civic society.

## Introduction

Government policies globally emphasise graduate employability as a key performance indicator for universities (Divan et al. 2019; Cameron, Farivar, and Coffey 2019). To meet the expected demand for knowledge workers to drive economic and social growth, policy makers have expanded higher education systems (Divan et al. 2019; Blackmore and Rahimi 2019). In Europe, the greater increase in graduates, linked to sluggish economic growth, has led to rising graduate unemployment (Eurostat 2019), and policies linked to graduate employment outcomes with base funding. Correspondingly, the Australian Government is compelling universities to take responsibility for the 'employability' of their graduates. Following recent higher education reform, the 'job-ready graduates' policy has tied graduate employment to a portion of university funding (Harvey et al. 2017; Karp 2020). Furthermore, fees for science, maths, engineering and health disciplines have decreased, while the humanities, like Creative Industries, have seen a 100 per cent increase (Karp 2020).

The dominance of the economic paradigm, marketisation of the educational systems, and narrow unsophisticated employment measures have been severely criticised by scholars (Bennett 2019; Christie 2017; Jackson and Bridgstock 2018). Skeggs (2014) argues that these policies aim to position students as rational investors in their education, over-emphasising individual economic gain from higher education qualifications and compelling them to think of themselves as solely economic contributors to the country's gross domestic product. Her position aligns with what Habermas (1987, 154) identifies as the repurposing of higher education to support '*the system* ... guided by economic acquisition and administering and controlling power'.

The economising of the academy does not bode well for the Creative Industries. This sector is significant in terms of employment and economic value (EY 2015; Jones, Lorenzen, and Sapsed 2015; Li 2020). The UK creative industries (CI) contributed £115.9bn in 2019 and grew by 43.6% between 2010 and 2019 in real terms (DCMS 2019). Similarly, in Australia the Cultural and Creative Industries contributed AU $111.7 billion to Australia's economy in 2016–2017, equivalent to 6.4 per cent of Australia's GDP.[1] Yet employment in this sector is precarious as self-employment and micro-firms employing less than five people dominate (Li 2020).

Despite these realities, CI degrees are often criticised for failing to deliver adequate employment prospects. Concerns regarding the oversupply of CI graduates are accompanied by concerns that once in the workforce, graduates will be unable to sustain careers in their preferred creative occupations (Bridgstock and Cunningham 2016). Despite this, CI graduates are embedded across a variety of employment sectors (Bridgstock et al. 2015), highlighting CI graduates' ability to add value to diverse national and international industries. As the CI are categorised by precarious employment and portfolio career structures (Hooley and Dodd 2015), CI programmes need to prepare students for careers in both 'specialist' and 'embedded' creative work opportunities within a precarious employment sector, while considering Habermas (1987) guidance.

An alternative to the economic paradigm of higher education is the view that the academy ought to support citizenship. In this paper *citizenship* refers to 'fellow-feeling' and participating responsibly and contributing to society, and whilst it can include self-interest, is opposed to selfishness and individualism, or inflicting harm (Obeng-Odoom 2019). Habermas (1987) argues that citizenship, or engaging in the 'lifeworld', requires critical thinking skills but adds that it ought to include public communication capabilities so graduates can communicate with wide audiences, and generate rational and valid insights, which should in turn inform public debate and policy.

We argue that as university curricula are leading indicators of changing ideological shifts in government power and socio-political priorities (Krause 2020), CI curriculum designers and academics should design curricula that both develop graduate employability (serving the system) and citizenship (serving lifeworlds), as these paradigms need not be positioned in opposition. Indeed, Barnett (2000a) identifies that universities operate within an era of supercomplexity, constituted by the co-existence of a multiplicity of frameworks 'where one is faced with a surfeit of data, knowledge or theoretical frames within one's immediate situation' (6). Barnett's (2000a, 2000b) notion of supercomplexity suggests that rather than presenting differing frames as mutually exclusive, they can be understood as a pattern of ideas and possibilities on which students can draw to make sense of an increasingly complex and precarious world (Bengtsen 2018). In this regard, graduate employability and citizenship are not paradoxical, merely two of several differing frames through which to engage.

In this paper, we investigate how to develop CI curricula that foster employability and citizenship. Firstly, we look at the CI's role against Barnett's (2000a) theory that the contemporary academy operates within an epoch of supercomplexity and how students can be supported to navigate 'the system' of CI employability, whilst simultaneously facilitating 'lifeworld' engaged citizenship. We then address the question of how to structure CI curriculum in practice to develop employability and citizenship, through an illustrative case study of a Bachelor of Creative Industries Program (BCI) at a regional Australian university.

## The creative industries and the role of higher education in supporting student employability in an era of supercomplexity

The neoliberalisations of market economies, disassembly of social support structures, and normalisation of labour flexibility policies have facilitated the relocation of production and employment to where costs are lowest (Standing 2011). In this context, precarity comes to be conceptualised as an emerging abandonment that pushes us away from 'a livable life' (Butler 2009, 25). The precarious livelihoods and working conditions of creative industries workers are widely acknowledged (Li 2020; Morgan and Nelligan 2018). Work in the Creative Industries is typically non-linear, with employment opportunities often created through single projects, self-devised activities, and informal networks (Daniel and Daniel 2015). The combination of flexibility and portfolio versatility with individuals increasingly undertaking numerous short-term roles means that there is a greater need for individuals to better self-manage their non-linear, precarious careers (Hooley and Dodd 2015). Precarity in the creative industries is further complicated by the individual passion and pleasure derived from producing creative goods, alongside the social value associated with artistry. This makes creative industries workers vulnerable to internalising and devaluing their skills, knowledge, and time (Caves 2003; Morgan and Nelligan 2018).

Alongside these pressures on the Creative Industries sector, higher education institutions face pressure from employers to ensure that graduates are sufficiently skilled and capable of undertaking roles within the new economy (Harvey et al. 2017). Correspondingly, governments exert power through policies forcing universities to take responsibility for the 'employability' of their graduates, with little regard for economic conditions (see Jackson and Bridgstock 2018). More broadly, Divan et al. (2019) note that universities are pressurised to operate in marketized systems, while a portion of university funding is tied to crude measures of graduate employment (Harvey et al. 2017; Karp 2020). These powerful forces take a narrow view of universities as instruments in the economy, rather than its broader social role which enable individuals to achieve their creative potential and contribute to a diverse, more socially just society (McArthur

2011). Furthermore, Tomaszewski et al. (2021) add higher education policies should consider the need for all graduates to make the transition from university to employment regardless of their socio-economic status or origins. Despite the criticisms levelled against the concept of 'employability', it has become a mainstay of government policy covering education, work and culture (Higdon 2018) and generally accepted to mean the capacity and potential of a graduate to secure employment (Yorke 2006).

Higher education's strategic priority of enhancing employability (Tomlinson 2012) means the sector must contribute to career development learning (CDL), enabling graduates to navigate contemporary workforces and increase their chances of career success (Jackson and Edgar 2019). Indeed, Jackson and Edgar (2019) suggest that students in non-vocational areas may need more encouragement to engage with CDL than those enrolled in vocationally focused programmes. Bridgstock et al. (2015) argue that fostering graduate employability within Creative Industries programmes is of paramount importance as:

> creative graduates can struggle through an extended education to work transition involving episodes of unpaid work experience and internships, additional education or training, and reliance on family, social security and/or 'day jobs' for financial support. (Bridgstock et al. 2015, 335)

Relatedly, Bridgstock (2009) establishes that tertiary providers can support employability by providing graduates with skills sought by employers, including both discipline-specific skills and transferable skills, including career management skills.

Yet, despite the pressure to support CDL for graduate employability within higher education, we are encouraged to resist the co-opting of tertiary education to promote neoliberalism. Zepke (2015) cautions against the appropriation of higher education to propagate neoliberalism generally and the 'individualist turn' specifically. The individualist turn situates employability, and the benefits thereof, as the responsibility of the individual and in so doing eschews the notion that one's employment might also be both dependent upon and designed to serve others (Crimmins 2020). The individualist turn and the appropriation of higher education to serve the economy align with what Habermas describes as 'the system', a space guided by economic acquisition and administering and controlling power (1987, 154). For Habermas (1987), the system continually attempts to dominate the lifeworld, what he describes as a public sphere or 'a realm of our social life in which something approaching public opinion can be formed', where people behave like citizens with 'the freedom to express and publish their opinions' (Habermas 1989, 136). The public sphere is also a democratic space in which public opinion is formed through a process of 'tasks of criticism' (Habermas 1989, 136). In this regard, universities can be agents of the lifeworld by facilitating students' sense of curiosity, knowledge development, and capacity and confidence to communicate and critique (Lawless 2017).

Within this discursive terrain, CI educationalists responsible for developing and facilitating curricular are faced with these two imperatives – to enhance student employability and support students' critical thinking so that they can make informed and critical contributions to the public communication sphere. However, such dichotomisation undermines the 'supercomplexity' of twenty-first Century knowledge systems.

Barnett (2000a) suggests that contemporary universities operate in an era of supercomplexity or as an 'epistemological hinterland' where knowledge boundaries are dislodged, and the notion that there is a 'right' form of knowing is critiqued. He also posits that within an epoch of supercomplexity, deep disciplinary knowledge creation, student-centred pedagogies, and adherence to economic and social policy are all simultaneously realisable. More recently Barnett (2018) has embraced an ecological view as universities are interconnected with the external world, not only economically, socially, culturally and ethically, but in reciprocal ways in that universities can shape their environments. Given that universities function as ecosystems, staff and students can actively engage and shape curricula responding to the social and economic effects of precarity, as these forces 'flow into each other' (9). Yet, as supercomplexity is 'a higher order form of complexity' students need frameworks to help them navigate the multifarious epistemologies and policy contexts in circulation (Barnett 2000a, 76). Barnett (2000b, 409) specifically contends that for students 'to make sense of the knowledge mayhem, and ... to enable [them] to live purposefully' they need to adopt an epistemology for living amid uncertainty.

In the next section, we present an illustrative case study of a Bachelor of Creative Industries programme curriculum to address the research question of how to structure the curriculum in practice to develop employability and citizenship. As such Barnett's theorisation of supercomplexity in concert with a Habermasian conceptual frame are employed. The case does not seek to reconcile the seemingly contrasting epistemological frameworks, but instead seeks, through applying Habermas's (1987) conceptions of 'the system' and 'lifeworld', to offer students an understanding of how they can simultaneously operationalise their critical thinking and public communication capacities in their future work roles.

## Illustrative case study

This paper employs an illustrative case study. Illustrative case studies are primarily descriptive and serve to make the unfamiliar familiar, providing rich descriptions and giving readers a common language about the topic in question (Kyburz-Graber 2004). An illustrative case adds in-depth insights and benefits from the prior development of theoretical arguments (Blomdahl 2019). Illustrative case findings provide useful heuristics to stimulate analysis within corresponding cases and encourage future research.

The case focuses on curriculum design of a Creative Industries Bachelor program (a BCI) at a regional university in Australia. Followed by a brief overview of the context of 'the case' (the BCI), we thematically analysed how key initiatives of the BCI curriculum align with Habermas's (1987) theoretical propositions regarding the system (Braun and Clarke 2006), and which are particularly designed to support individual employability. Next, key features of the case which both constitute and support 'the lifeworld' and citizenship (Habermas 1987) are elucidated. Finally, we consider how CI graduates might simultaneously serve the system, though engaging in paid employment, whilst creating inclusive and progressive public communications, via creative artefacts, which can serve the lifeworld.

### Context of the case

The University of the Sunshine Coast (USC) is one of Australia's fastest-growing public universities, opening its first campus in 1996 with 524 students, expanding to almost

18,112 students in 2020 (USC 2020). It is a regional university with most of its campuses located in geographical areas with a small number of large employers, and most of the population around its larger campuses self-employed, working for small firms, non-profit organisations, or as public-sector employees. In Semester One of 2020 there were 389 student enrolments in a Bachelor of Creative Industries (BCI). BCI is a three-year flexible degree programme that has been offered at the University of the Sunshine Coast since 2014.

While university student enrolments in Australia have increased in recent years, in metropolitan and regional and remote areas, the basic inequality in education participation prevails (Shoemaker 2017). In 2016, 42 per cent of people aged 25–34 in major cities held a Bachelor's degree, compared to 19 per cent in regional Australia (Australian Bureau of Statistics 2017). Although there has been some improvement in the proportion of low socio-economic status (LSES) students attending university, the proportion of regional students has not significantly changed. Data reveals that people from major cities are twice as likely to hold a degree than those from regional and remote areas, and students at regional universities are more likely to identify as LSES and mature age. These elements are reflected in the profile of USC students. The student population within USC's School of Creative Industries is characterised by a large percentage of non-traditional students, with 57 per cent identifying as female, and over 40 per cent of students the first in their family to enrol into a university programme. Graduate employment after graduation is a major challenge for students within USC, with 58 per cent of students securing full time employment upon graduation, compared to the national average of 71.5 per cent, and graduates' average salary of $62,000 compares unfavourably with the national graduate average of $68,000 (USC, Student Statistical Summary 2020). Within USC's BCI, students undertake an eight-subject major and four-subject minor, choosing from a wide range of complementary disciplines to access a combination that best suits their interests and career goals.

### Curriculum design to support graduate employability (the system)

The design of the BCI is informed by the core skills and competencies required to practice as a professional in the Creative Industries, including career management within a highly precarious industry sector. Many professionals in the Creative Industries undertake 'portfolio careers' that combine creative and non-creative jobs, and employment is short-term, project-based, and self-generated (Bridgstock 2005). There are various perspectives as to why this is the case. For instance, Morgan, Wood, and Nelligan (2013) suggest that many young CI workers choose portfolio work because it is liberating and adaptive. This perspective supports organisation and workplace literature that identifies that workers have agency in choosing to pursue protean careers where workplace gratification is deemed more important than regular income (Gerli, Bonesso, and Claudio 2015). Yet, there is paradoxical evidence that suggests creatives adopt portfolio working arrangements out of financial necessity (Bridgstock et al. 2015).

Additionally, despite the Good Universities Guide (2019) identifying that USC ranked as the second-worst university in Queensland for graduates gaining full-time employment within four months of completing their course, USC is considered one of the top universities in Australia in terms of providing graduates with the industry-specific skills that employers need. The National Employer Satisfaction Survey (2018) shows that USC ranked third out of 41 institutions for 'overall satisfaction', which measures the likelihood of employers considering hiring another graduate from the same course and institution. There is thus a substantial disconnect between the workplace-ready competencies USC students possess, and their lack of entry into employment. This suggests a need to connect and align students' competencies with their ability to identify and access employment opportunities. The following curriculum-based initiatives were introduced across the BCI undergraduate programme to support graduate employability, which are aligned with 'the system' (the economy).

Responding to graduate employability needs of (largely) non-traditional learners within a precarious sector, curricula were designed to support students to identify work opportunities, foster career aspirations, build a peer and industry network, and construct social and digital connectedness and Web 2.0 capabilities. Through the lens of supercomplexity, CI graduates need to exhibit graduate employability competencies in order to apply their critical thinking, public communication competencies, and citizenship through paid employment. Transdisciplinary competencies and skills are also required for graduate success to respond to the increasingly dynamic career landscape. Specific initiatives include: Establishing a Facebook group 'Guest of the week' to provide students with mentorship and introduce them to new possibilities of creative projects and work with which they may not yet be familiar; Facilitating students to undertake a 'skills, qualities, connections audit' in relation to a role or project in the CIs to which they aspire to help them develop 'a sense of purpose' (also supports student retention); Setting students the task of creating a digital profile through which to showcase their skills, interests and career aspirations, and support digital networking; Providing students with a video series of lectures as re-usable learning resources to encourage student engagement; and Work integrated learning projects designed to support students' development of professional networks and social ties to assist their employability.

### Facebook group 'Guest of the week'

Most students at USC are considered non-traditional learners, as they are over 21, and many are the first in their family to attend university and/or LSES. It is known that underrepresentation in graduate employment is often due in part to the social disadvantage non-traditional students experience. Specifically, students' aspirations are adapted to fit what seems preferable and achievable to them (Gale and Parker 2017). This phenomenon, known as adaptive preference, suggests that students' preferences and behaviours are shaped by what appears to be available (Doughney 2007). Thus, tertiary students cannot prefer or pursue an employment option if they do not know about it, or they believe is not available to them or 'people like them'. To redress the structural conditions that can restrict student employability of non-traditional students, a group was created on the social media platform Facebook for a first semester, first-year introductory unit that is a compulsory within BCI. Local, national, and international industry practitioners in the Creative Industries were invited to join the group. The practitioners become 'Guests of the Week' in the Facebook group and answer student questions, discuss their own career journeys, and offer career advice and mentorship. This initiative explicitly demonstrates to students the work/project opportunities that are available, and that the practitioners are 'people like them', often from non-traditional learner backgrounds themselves. The use of a social media interface means that students across several regional campuses can regularly connect with one another *and* with local, national, and international practitioners. The life stories that these professionals share facilitate the development of students' aspirations whilst providing practical advice on how to be successful within their disciplinary field.

### Skills, qualities and connections audit

Student attrition is a significant problem at USC. In 2018 USC's attrition rate was 22.3 per cent – one of the highest for Queensland, Australia (and Queensland had the second highest attrition rate of all Australasian states and territories). Lizzio and Wilson's (2013) seminal research on student engagement identified that 'a sense of purpose' is a key predictor of success at university, and that students who have a clear career or post-university goal are far more likely to complete tertiary study. The BCI curricula was designed to help students identify a career goal/post-study aspiration, by introducing a 'skills, qualities and connections' audit as the first assessment task in the compulsory first-year unit. The task requires students to locate a job advertisement or project work in their field for which they would ideally like to apply or would like to complete upon completion of their programme. The students then assess their current level of skills, qualities and connections against those they would need to successfully apply for the position. Finally, students create a professional development plan for themselves that identifies what units, work experience, qualities, and networking experience they will need in order to be application-ready upon graduating. This approach differs from most programmes within which students are provided 'just in time' career advice and support during their final year of study.

### Digital profile

Social and digital connectedness and Web 2.0 capabilities are increasingly important for gaining graduate employment (Bridgstock and Cunningham 2016). These competencies require both an entrepreneurial mindset and the confidence and ability to use social networking sites, such as LinkedIn, to connect with potential collaborators and employers, to learn about job vacancies, and to showcase and promote one's skills and qualities. Yet, evidence from recent research undertaken at USC identifies that while 57 per cent of USC students have a LinkedIn profile, only 25.2 per cent of students' profiles are up to date and over two-fifths of students do not have a LinkedIn profile (De Villiers-Scheepers et al. 2019). To support students to create a digital profile/portfolio this was introduced as the final assessment task in the first-year compulsory introductory BCI unit. Students created a discipline-appropriate profile/portfolio format (e.g. Vimeo account, website, LinkedIn profile, personal blog) to present and promote their personal narratives, projects and skills. They were also required to create a map of local work experience, internship, or volunteering opportunities in their field, and develop a communication text (email or phone interview transcript) to introduce themselves to prospective collaborators or employers, within which they list the link to their digital profile.

## Video series

One of the most significant barriers to student learning at university, before the widespread adoption of online learning tools during and post COVID-19, was that many students fail to engage fully with lecture content. Live lecture attendance data at USC identified that one in five students miss one or more classes per week due to work commitments, a finding which aligns with national trends (Chapin 2018). Nevertheless, students increasingly watch lectures online via the institutional Mediasite, which is a capture tool that records live lectures and makes the recordings available online. In these recordings, the lecturer's voice can be heard as the relevant lecture slides are presented full-screen and a small, inset window displays a long-distance (often blurry) image of the lecturer presenting. In response – long before COVID-19 required the widespread embrace of online learning across high education institutions – a lecture series was redesigned of a compulsory BCI unit creating dynamic lecture videos featuring interviews with Creative Industries discipline leads and industry professionals. Examples: *The Creative Process* (https://youtu.be/nFDOXOt9QWE); *Audience* (https://youtu.be/B_BTcmRiqNo; and *Design* (https://youtu.be/Px-XIOrerbM). Within the video series close-up, 'humanised' conversations were presented that capture the presenters' gestures and facial expressions, as opposed to static Mediasite recordings of tiny bodies and large PowerPoints. The significance of this research-informed online lecture series lies in its capacity to support students to engage in humanistic learning experiences via technologically enabled learning resources that fit around students' other work and study commitments, corresponding to students' behaviour regarding online learning. Over 90 per cent of students enrolled in the unit in Semester Two, 2019 watched each video set. Considering significant pivots to online learning in 2020 due to the COVID-19 pandemic, the relevance and necessity of the effectiveness of online lectures has become even more pronounced.

## Work-integrated learning (WIL) initiatives

In the changing world of employment, careers are increasingly mobile and flexible, which requires workers to have established professional networks and social ties (Lochab and Mor 2013). Furthermore, networking capabilities and a strong portfolio are especially important for creative professionals, as a significant proportion is employed in industries outside the core creative industries as 'embedded creatives' (Goldsmith and Bridgstock 2015). In order to address this need, within all eleven majors offered in the BCI, industry professionals were engaged as instructors and guest lecturers in all 200 and 300 level units, incorporate work integrated learning (WIL) or internship opportunities, and encourage student collaboration. It is also recognised that at least a third of university students do not feel prepared for a career upon graduation. In order to better prepare students before they head out into the contemporary world of work, the BCI capstone unit provides students with the opportunity to consolidate the knowledge and professional skills they have gained throughout their programme while further developing their professional networks. To do so, a selection of on-campus WIL projects was offered in addition to off-campus internships.

When undertaking the on-campus projects, students work in groups to industry standards to devise and execute projects while working with industry-active mentors. They produce a high-quality artefact to include in their portfolio. Interdisciplinary project opportunities were also offered, encouraging students from across different majors to collaborate. Relationships with local and national industry partners provided the opportunity to offer students a variety of internships placements. Students collaborating on real-world projects enhance their career preparedness and help them expand their professional networks and social connections. Creating high quality artefacts enables students to further expand their portfolio, which they can then use to gain employment once graduated. Internship placements are significant because they develop students' industry connections and provide authentic learning and real-world work experiences. Hence, many features of the BCI focus on supporting students' career development and enhancing their graduate employability, thus aligning with Habermas's (1984; 1987) notion of the system, as they are guided by economic acquisition.

### Curriculum design to support the lifeworld

Through the BCI, conditions were created conducive to students' developing critical thinking and public communication skills, which provide them with opportunities to engage in what Habermas terms the lifeworld. Learning environments were designed in which public opinion is formed through a process of 'tasks of criticism' (Habermas 1987, 136) and in which communicative competence is fostered.

The BCI were redesigned with specific features to support students' critical, communication and citizenship faculties as they learn to develop public facing communications/artefacts in screen media, theatre performances, music and creative writing. CI students intend to design and develop public-facing creative artefacts. These artefacts might be screen media content, theatre performances, novels, short stories, music, podcasts etc. Students therefore present to the world, either consciously or unconsciously, their world views in the form and through the content of their creative artefact. In doing so creative artists might hegemonically re-present and reinforce existing ideologies (that are often saturated with neo-liberal, nationalistic, homophobic, racist, sexist, ageist and ableist connotation and impact). Alternatively, creatives who are aware of the social and political significance of the communication signals (signs) they use in their work, and who consider what key messages and representations their work inhabits, have the capacity to make manifest alternative and more progressive and inclusive ideologies. That is, people working in CI can create worlds that show us what is possible, probable, just, and fair; they can show us how to be, and how/why not to be. CI professionals are thus powerful culture-makers.

To support students to become cognisant of their power and responsibility as culture makers, learning opportunities were developed that align with Habermas's (1987) notion of the lifeworld, which includes narrative, persona, orientation and affinity, and emancipatory paradigm, which encourages critical thinking and action in relation to all aspects of society and culture. The emancipatory paradigm 'mandates critiques of oppression, power imbalances and undemocratic practices' (Zepke 2015, 1316) and facilitates a critical consciousness that encourages social and political action (Stuckey et al. 2015). The focus of the paradigm is critical action designed to recognise and combat inequities and achieve greater social justice. In order to actualise this emancipatory paradigm, a 13-week introductory unit was developed that familiarises first-year students with semiology (the study of signs and sign systems) and the processes of using signs to create and share meaning. In this unit, students were given the tools with which to identify and deconstruct individual and cultural connotations of signs, and to determine how sign systems can support social hierarchies and justify the domination of certain social groups through the processes such as hegemony (Gramsci 1971), exnomination (Barthes 2009), surveillance (Foucault 1975), and gender performativity (Butler 1990). Engaging with carefully developed curriculum, students examine the ways discourses and ideologies circulate and construct meaning, and how they maintain broader socio-political power. This curriculum provides opportunities for students to examine how media representations reflect and affect dominant discourses and ideologies. For example, students are required (in an assessment) to present an analysis of a chosen media text, applying theories studied in the unit to evaluate the extent to which it can be understood to offer a model for social change and/or to reinforce oppressive ideologies.

Furthermore, a significant aspect to a second year BCI unit offered introduces critical theories and ideas about why and how to create original counter-hegemonic creative artefacts that introduce new or progressive discourses and ideologies into society, and which challenge the status quo and dominant world view. Within the unit students are provided with definitions, explanations and examples of critical theories embedded in creative works. These include feminisms, masculinities, ethnicity and colonialism (including cultural colonisation), eurocentrism, post-colonialism, gender and sexualities. Throughout a series of lectures and corresponding tutorial activities students interrogate how creative texts can be oppressive by denying voice to certain groups, negative/diminishing or stereotypical representation, and discriminatory symbols and language. They also examine how these texts can be reformative by giving voice and visibility, reclaiming symbols and language, extending who 'writes' or 'makes' the story, not just about whom the story is told. Students are required to critically analyse representation/s within texts but also develop new creative texts alongside an analysis of who is/is not included, the diversity of characteristics given to characters, what ideologies and ideas/discourses they build into their work, and its cultural/political aim. After providing students with the frames of reference and languages creative artefact makes, they are invited to create original counter-hegemonic creative artefacts that introduce new or progressive discourses and ideologies into society, and which challenge the status quo and dominant world view. Following on from and scaffolding this learning, a third-year unit further extends students' critical thinking through project or WIL opportunities. In these ways, the BCI supports Creative Industries graduates to critically evaluate public creative and communication texts, develop a capacity to design and craft creative artefacts that inhabit progressive and inclusive public communications, to recognise their role and responsibility as culture-makers and contribute to the citizenship of the lifeworld.

## Implications for curriculum designers

The case of BCI curriculum design that embraces ecological supercomplexity by attending to graduate employability and students' critical thinking and public communication competencies illustrates how curriculum initiatives can be structured to address these distinct challenges. By embracing Barnett's (2018) claim that the twenty-first Century is characterised by supercomplexity, we recognise the complex reciprocal interactions of social and economic effects of precarity, as well as the acceleration and intensification of time in relation to labour by developing a variety of different skills among CI graduates in the production of creative work. Thus CI graduates can simultaneously contribute to the lifeworld by creating inclusive and progressive public communications and creative artefacts to inform debate and culture, whilst pursuing or engaging in paid employment which forms part of the system. Indeed, Barnett (1997) suggests that the development of diverse knowledge practices involving in-depth questioning and scholarly inquiry is integral to – and not separate from – the employability and leadership capacities of university graduates. Danvers (2016, 283) similarly proposes that critical thinking 'shifts in accordance with the social, embodied and relational contexts', and Barnett (2000a, 21) argues:

> we should think of the university as engaged in knowledge processes in different knowledge settings, exploiting knowledge possibilities. Some of these processes and some of these settings will, it is hoped, yield capital of some kind: to the attractiveness of intellectual capital has been added financial and symbolic capital.

We therefore argue that CI graduates might operate the system whilst resisting its domination of the lifeworld, *if* they are guided to handle 'multiple frames of understanding, of action and of self-identity' (Barnett 2000a, 6) (our emphasis). This requires CI academics who lead university units, programmes, and units of work to clearly (and iteratively) articulate and demonstrate to students that they are studying/living amid times of economic uncertainty and increasing precarity and epistemological plurality. Learning leaders are be encouraged to develop curricula designed to support students 'to make sense of the knowledge mayhem, and … to enable [them] to live purposefully [by providing them with the opportunity to develop] … an epistemology for living amid uncertainty' (409). Beyond CI curriculum developers this paper also hold implications for other humanities disciplines, given the importance to develop both employability and citizenship to facilitate a thriving civil society where members can respectfully debate societal issues, contribute to the economy and volunteer contributions to facilitate a more inclusive and just society.

## Conclusion

Graduates require networks, confidence and the adaptability to cope with uncertain, dynamic employment contexts, as they transition to the world-of-work. This is particularly true for CI graduates who undertake qualifications in a sector characterised by precarity and portfolio careers. Hitherto, the focus on employability within the Creative Industries and higher education systems has been demarcated from discourses of graduate citizenship. In this paper we integrate these two key aspects of university curricula (graduate employability and critical thinking and communication) understood to serve Habermas (1987) notion of *the system* and *the lifeworld* respectively. Using Barnett's (2000b; 2018) framework of supercomplexity, we shared a case study of a Bachelor of Creative Industries programme to illustrate how curricula can support students to navigate both the system and the lifeworld simultaneously. Finally, we encourage leaders in learning and teaching to develop curricula to support students to manage diverse and seemingly paradoxical ideas, ways of knowing and working, and imperatives so that they can adopt individually meaningful and culturally engaged lifeworlds.

This paper does not offer empirical generalisability, as it uses a single cross-sectional case study, which renders the representativeness and transferability of the case study relatively limited. Future research should engage with a wider cross-section of curricula, across multiple university settings, would address some of these limitations. This study aimed to stimulate discussion among other academics and curriculum developers. Finally, we suggest that in order to support future Creative Industries citizens, university curricula should prepare students to effectively navigate across multiple sectors, industries, careers and ideological geographies.

## Note

1. Cultural and creative activity can be measured separately or as both cultural and creative activity. Cultural activity contributed AU$63.5 billion or 3.6 per cent to GDP in 2016–2017, while creative activity contributed AU$99.7 billion or 5.7 per cent to GDP in 2016–2017. There is considerable overlap of industries and occupations common with these segments. Activity that has identified as both cultural and creative accounted for AU$51.5 billion or 3.0 per cent to GDP (Australian Government 2019).

## Disclosure statement

No potential conflict of interest was reported by the author(s).

## ORCID

*Gail Crimmins* ⓘ http://orcid.org/0000-0002-7548-0139
*Joanna McIntyre* ⓘ http://orcid.org/0000-0003-1909-5997
*Margarietha de Villiers Scheepers* ⓘ http://orcid.org/0000-0002-5084-854X

## References

Australian Bureau of Statistics. 2017. *Enrolled Fulltime Aboriginal and Torres Strait Islander Students, by States and Territories 2016*. http://www.abs.gov.au/ausstats/abs@.nsf/mf/4221.0.

Australian Government, Department of Communications and the Arts. Bureau of Communications and Arts Research. 2019. *Creative Skills for the Future Economy*. http://hdl.voced.edu.au/10707/500287.

Barnett, Ronald. 1997. *Higher Education: A Critical Business*. Buckingham: SHRE and Open University Press.

Barnett, Ronald. 2000a. *Realizing the University in an Age of Supercomplexity*. Buckingham: Open University Press.

Barnett, Ronald. 2000b. "Supercomplexity and the Curriculum." *Studies in Higher Education* 25 (3): 255–265. doi:10.1080/713696156.

Barnett, Ronald. 2018. *The Ecological University: A Feasible Utopia*. Abingdon: Routledge.

Barthes, Roland. 2009. *Mythologies*. London: Vintage.

Bengtsen, Søren SE. 2018. "Supercomplexity and the University: Ronald Barnett and the Social Philosophy of Higher Education." *Higher Education Quarterly* 72 (1): 65–74. doi:10.1111/hequ.12153.

Bennett, Dawn. 2019. "Meeting Society's Expectations of Graduates: Education for the Public Good." In *Education for Employability 1: Learning for Future Possibilities*, edited by Joy Higgs, Will Letts, and Geoffrey Crisps, 35–48. Rotterdam: Brill.

Blackmore, Jill, and Mark Rahimi. 2019. "How 'Best Fit' Excludes International Graduates from Employment in Australia: A Bourdeusian Perspective." *Journal of Education and Work* 32 (5): 436–448. doi:10.1080/13639080.2019.1679729.

Blomdahl, Mikael. 2019. "Changing the Conversation in Washington? An Illustrative Case Study of President Trump's Air Strikes on Syria, 2017." *Diplomacy & Statecraft* 30 (3): 536–555. doi:10.1080/09592296.2019.1641924.

Braun, Virginia, and Victoria Clarke. 2006. "Using Thematic Analysis in Psychology." *Qualitative Research in Psychology* 3 (2): 77–101.

Bridgstock, Ruth. 2005. "Australian Artists, Starving and Well-Nourished: What Can we Learn from the Prototypical Protean Career?" *Australian Journal of Career Development* 14 (3): 40–48. doi:10.1177/103841620501400307.

Bridgstock, R. 2009. "The Graduate Attributes We've Overlooked: Enhancing Graduate Employability Through Career Management Skills." *Higher Education Research & Development* 28 (1): 31–44. doi:10.1080/07294360802444347.

Bridgstock, Ruth, Goldsmith Ben, Jess Rodgers, and Gregg Hearn. 2015. "Creative Graduate Pathways Within and Beyond the Creative Industries." *Journal of Education and Work* 28 (4): 333–345. doi:10.1080/13639080.2014.997682.

Bridgstock, Ruth, and Stuart Cunningham. 2016. "Creative Labour and Graduate Outcomes: Implications for Higher Education and Cultural Policy." *International Journal of Cultural Policy* 22 (1): 10–26. doi:10.1080/10286632.2015.1101086.

Butler, Judith. 1990. *Gender Trouble*. New York: Routledge.

Butler, Judith. 2009. *"Performativity, Precarity, Sexual Politics."* AIBR *Revista de Antropología Iberoamericana* 4 (3): i–xii.

Cameron, Roslyn, Farveh Farivar, and Jane Coffey. 2019. "International Graduates Host Country Employment Intentions and Outcomes: Evidence from two Australian Universities." *Journal of Higher Education Policy and Management* 41 (5): 550–568. doi:10.1080/1360080X.2019. 1646383.

Caves, Richard. 2003. "Contracts Between Art and Commerce." *The Journal of Economic Perspectives* 17 (2): 73–84. doi:10.1257/089533003765888430.

Chapin, Laurie. 2018. "Australian University Students' Access to web-Based Lecture Recordings and the Relationship with Lecture Attendance and Academic Performance." *Australasian Journal of Educational Technology* 34 (5), Doi: 10.14742/ajet.2989.

Christie, Fiona. 2017. "The Reporting of University League Table Employability Rankings: A Critical Review." *Journal of Education and Work* 30 (4): 403–418. doi:10.1080/13639080.2016. 1224821.

Crimmins, Gail. 2020. "Don't Throw out the Baby with the Bathwater: Statistics Can Create Impetus to Address Educational Inequity." In *Strategies for Supporting Inclusion and Diversity in the Academy*, edited by G. Crimmins, 3–26. Cham: Palgrave Macmillan.

Daniel, R., and L. Daniel. 2015. "Success in the Creative Industries: The Push for Enterprising and Entrepreneurial Skills." *Journal of Australian Studies* 39 (3): 411–424. doi:10.1080/14443058. 2015.1046896.

Danvers, Emily. 2016. "Criticality's Affective Entanglements: Rethinking Emotion and Critical Thinking in Higher Education." *Gender and Education* 28 (2): 282–297. doi:10.1080/ 09540253.2015.1115469.

DCMS (Department for Digital, Culture Media and Sport). 2019. *DCMS Economic Estimates 2019 (provisional): Gross Value Added.* https://www.gov.uk/government/statistics/dcms-economic-estimates-2019-gross-value-added/dcms-economic-estimates-2019-provisional-gross-value-added.

De Villiers-Scheepers, M. J., Joanna McIntyre, Gail Crimmins, and Peter English. 2019. "Connectedness Capabilities of Non-traditional Students: Pedagogical Implications." In *Higher Education and the Future of Graduate Employability: A Connectedness Learning Approach*, edited by Ruth Bridgstoc, and Neil Tippett, 59–60. Cheltenham: Edward Elgar.

Divan, Aysha, Elizabeth Knight, Dawn Bennett, and Kenton Bell. 2019. "Marketing Graduate Employability: Understanding the Tensions Between Institutional Practice and External Messaging." *Journal of Higher Education Policy and Management* 41 (5): 485–499. doi:10. 1080/1360080X.2019.1652427.

Doughney, J. 2007. "Women and Leadership in Corporate Australia: Questions of Preference and "Adaptive Preference"." *Advancing Women in Leadership* 23: 1–10.

Eurostat. 2019. *Employment Rates of Recent Graduates.* https://ec.europa.eu/eurostat/web/ products-datasets/-/tps00053.

EY. 2015. "Cultural Times – The First Global Map of Cultural and Creative Industries." *Ernst & Young Global.* http://www.ey.com/Publication/vwLUAssets/ey-cultural-times-2015/ $FILE/ey-cultural-times-2015.pdf.

Foucault, Michel. 1975. *Discipline and Punish*. London: Penguin.

Gale, Trevor, and Stephen Parker. 2017. "Retaining Students in Australian Higher Education: Cultural Capital, Field Distinction." *European Educational Research Journal* 16 (1): 80–96. doi:10.1177/1474904116678004.

Gerli, Fabrizio, Sara Bonesso, and Pizzi Claudio. 2015. "Boundaryless Career and Career Success: The Impact of Emotional and Social Competencies." *Frontiers in Psychology* 6: 1304. doi:10. 3389/fpsyg.2015.01304.

Goldsmith, Ben, and Ruth Bridgstock. 2015. "Embedded Creative Workers and Creative Work in Education." *Journal of Education and Work* 28 (4): 369–387. doi:10.1080/13639080.2014.997684.

Good Universities Guide. 2019. https://www.goodeducation.com.au/gug/.

Gramsci, Antonio. 1971. *Selections from the Prison Notebooks of Antonio Gramsci*. London: Laurence and Wishart.

Habermas, Jürgen. 1984. *Reason and the Rationalization of Society. The Theory of Communicative Action, vol. 1*. Boston, MA: Beacon Press.

Habermas, Jürgen. 1987. *The Theory of Communicative Action. Volume 2 Lifeworld and System: The Critique of Functionalist Reason*. Translated by T McCarthy. Cambridge: Polity Press.

Habermas, J. 1989. *Structural Transformation of the Public Sphere*. Cambridge, MA: MIT Press.

Harvey, Andrew, Lisa Andrewartha, Daniel Edwards, Julia Clarke, and Kimberly Reyes. 2017. *Student Equity and Employability in Higher Education*. Report for the Australian Government Department of Education and Training. Melbourne: Centre for Higher Education Equity and Diversity Research, La Trobe University.

Higdon, Rachel. 2018. "From Employability to 'Complexability': Creatour – a Construct for Preparing Students for Creative Work and Life." *Industry and Higher Education* 32 (1): 33–46. doi:10.1177/0950422217744721.

Hooley, T., and V. Dodd. 2015. *The Economic Benefits of Career Guidance*. Careers England.

Jackson, Denise A, and Ruth Bridgstock. 2018. "Evidencing Student Success and Graduate Employability in the Contemporary World-of-Work: Renewing our Thinking." *Higher Education Research and Development* 37 (5): 984–988. doi:10.1080/07294360.2018.1469603.

Jackson, Denise A, and Susan Edgar. 2019. "Encouraging Students to Draw on Work Experiences When Articulating Achievements and Capabilities to Enhance Employability." *Australian Journal of Career Development* 28 (1): 39–50. doi:10.1177/1038416218790571.

Jones, Candace, Mark Lorenzen, and Jonathan Sapsed. 2015. "Creative Industries: A Typology of Change." *The Oxford Handbook of Creative Industries* 3: 32.

Karp, Paul. 2020. "Australian University Fees to Double for Some Arts Courses, but fall for Stem Subjects." *The Guardian*. https://www.theguardian.com/australia-news/2020/jun/19/australian-university-fees-arts-stem-science-maths-nursing-teaching-humanities.

Krause, Kerri-Lee D. 2020. "Vectors of Change in Higher Education Curricula." *Journal of Curriculum Studies*. doi:10.1080/00220272.2020.1764627.

Kyburz-Graber, Regula. 2004. "Does Case-Study Methodology Lack Rigour? The Need for Quality Criteria for Sound Case-Study Research, as Illustrated by a Recent Case in Secondary and Higher Education." *Environmental Education Research* 10 (1): 53–65. doi:10.1080/1350462032000173706.

Lawless, Ann. 2017. "Affirming Humanity: A Case Study of the Activism of General/Professional Staff in the Academy." *Australian Universities' Review* 59 (2): 50–58.

Li, Feng. 2020. "The Digital Transformation of Business Models in the Creative Industries: A Holistic Framework and Emerging Trends." *Technovation* 92: 102012. doi:10.1016/j.technovation.2017.12.004.

Lizzio, Alf, and Keithia Wilson. 2013. "Early Intervention to Support the Academic Recovery of First-Year Students at Risk of non-Continuation." *Innovations in Education and Teaching International* 50 (2): 109–120. doi:10.1080/14703297.2012.760867.

Lochab, Anshu, and Kiran Mor. 2013. "Traditional to Boundaryless Career: Redefining Career in 21st Century." *Global Journal of Management and Business Studies* 3 (5): 485–490.

McArthur, Jan. 2011. "Reconsidering the Social and Economic Purposes of Higher Education." *Higher Education Research & Development* 30 (6): 737–749. doi:10.1080/07294360.2010.539596.

Morgan, George, and Pariece Nelligan. 2018. *The Creativity Hoax: Precarious Work in the Gig Economy*. New York, NY: Anthem Press.

Morgan, G., J. Wood, and P. Nelligan. 2013. "Beyond the Vocational Fragments: Creative Work, Precarious Labour and the Idea of 'Flexploitation." *The Economic and Labour Relations Review* 24 (3): 397–415. doi:10.1177/1035304613500601.

The National Employer Satisfaction Survey. 2018. https://www.qilt.edu.au/qilt-surveys/employer-satisfaction.

Obeng-Odoom, Franklin. 2019. "Economics, Education, and Citizenship." *Australian Universities' Review* 61 (1): 3–11.

Shoemaker, A. 2017. "A New Approach to Regional Higher Education is Essential to Our Economic Future." The Conversation. https://theconversation.com/a-new-approach-to-regional-higher-education-is-essential-to-our-economic-future-88537.

Skeggs, Beverley. 2014. "Values Beyond Value? Is Anything Beyond the Logic of Capital?"." *British Journal of Sociology* 65 (1): 1–20. doi:10.1111/1468-4446.12072.

Standing, Guy. 2011. *The Precariat: The New Dangerous Class.* New York: Bloomsbury.

Stuckey, M., P. Heering, R. Mamlok-Naaman, A. Hofstein, and I. Eilks. 2015. "The Philosophical Works of Ludwik Fleck and Their Potential Meaning for Teaching and Learning Science." *Science & Education* 24 (3): 281–298.

Tomaszewski, Wojtek, Francisco Perales, Ning Xiang, and Matthias Kubler. 2021. "Beyond Graduation: Socio-Economic Background and Post-University Outcomes of Australian Graduates." *Research in Higher Education* 62: 26–44. doi:10.1007/s11162-019-09578-4.

Tomlinson, Michael. 2012. "Graduate Employability: A Review of Conceptual and Empirical Themes." *Higher Education Policy* 25 (4): 407–431. doi:10.1057/hep.2011.26.

University of the Sunshine Coast. 2020. *Student Statistical Summary* (unpublished).

Yorke, Mantz. 2006. *Employability in Higher Education: What it is – What it is not. Vol 1.* York: Higher Education Academy.

Zepke, Nick. 2015. "Student Engagement Research: Thinking Beyond the Mainstream." *Higher Education Research & Development* 34 (6): 1311–1323. doi:10.1080/07294360.2015.1024635.

# Ethical responsibilities of tenured academics supervising non-tenured researchers in times of neoliberalism and precarity

Kathleen Smithers [ID], Jess Harris [ID], Mhorag Goff [ID], Nerida Spina [ID] and Simon Bailey [ID]

**ABSTRACT**
Neoliberal reform of the university sector has resulted in increasing numbers of academics employed on casual or fixed-term contracts. While there is an emergent body of literature on issues of precarity in the academy, relatively little attention has been paid to the roles and responsibilities of those tenured academics who employ and *manage* non-tenured researchers. The work involved in hiring and managing a contract researcher is rarely acknowledged or supported, and managers receive little to no training. In this paper, we draw on Dorothy Smith's feminist sociological approach to analyse interviews with 22 non-tenured researchers to examine how managerial relationships shape the employment experiences of those working precariously. We argue that tenured academics have ethical responsibilities to provide a working environment that is fair, supports the ongoing development and wellbeing of non-tenured staff, and challenges dominant discourses of precarious academics as 'other'.

## Neoliberalism and the academy

Modern universities across much of the Western world have adapted to function in the context of neoliberalism. Reliance on student fees and research income, coupled with limitations in public funding, notably in the UK, the US, and Australia, have resulted in a significant shift in the focus of university management towards 'academic capitalism' (Deem et al. 2000; Slaughter and Rhoades 2004). In this context, the employment of permanent academic staff for research and teaching is both risky and costly.

The resulting decline in permanent academic positions is a global phenomenon (Acker and Haque 2017). The neoliberal project has paved the way for increasing responsibilisation of workers, as organisations have sought to shift risks and responsibilities from the organisation onto their employees (Lewchuk et al. 2003). Employees bear the risks associated with changing markets and the statutory and financial liabilities of the institution are limited (Brady and Briody 2016). A common approach adopted by universities is to unbundle integrated teaching and research positions, creating additional teaching-only and research-only positions (Holmwood and Servós 2019; Macfarlane 2011). In this way, non-tenured researchers (NTRs) are required to become entrepreneurial and secure employment that is often tethered to external research grants, for projects generally led by tenured academics (ILO 2019).

The terms 'non-tenured' and 'tenured' have been chosen to denote the diversity of positions within academia. Across Australia and the UK there are many differing terms regarding employment and employment conditions. Our use of the term 'non-tenured' is inclusive of academics working in casual or fixed term positions, while 'tenured' is used to identify those in ongoing employment. These broad descriptions are used to identify the emergence of a hierarchical 'tiered faculty', at the top of which are a privileged 'core' of tenured staff who are less susceptible to the precarity experienced by their colleagues on the 'tenuous periphery' (Holmwood and Servós 2019; Kimber 2003).

NTRs overwhelmingly report their relationships with managers are critical in their experiences in tenuous employment (Spina et al. 2020). While there is substantial literature on precarity as a sociological phenomenon and on precarious work (e.g. Baik, Naylor, and Corrin 2018; Ryan, Connell, and Burgess 2017; Stringer et al. 2018), little attention has been paid to the role of tenured managers of precarious employees. Drawing on interviews with 22 NTRs, we examine the nature of hierarchical relationships that exist within the neoliberal university and the ethical responsibilities adopted by managers in this system. We use descriptions of the 'everyday work' (Smith 2005) of these researchers as the *point d'appui* for our inquiry into how the relationships between NTRs and their managers shape the experiences of those in precarious employment. Given this theoretical standpoint, the perspectives described within the paper are drawn from the experiences of the researchers, rather than of the managers with whom they work. We have chosen to use the term 'manager' rather than 'supervisor' primarily to avoid potential confusion with the role of academic supervision, as conceived in higher degree research studies or post-doctoral programmes. Additionally, we eschew the term 'academic-managers' as this title infers a specific identity for individuals, who hold values that align with 'managerial discourse' (Winter 2009). Rather than adopting an *a priori* perception of managers and their values, we examine how management practices described by interviewed NTRs align with the tripartite framework of 'ethical leadership' described by Starratt (1991, 1996). The purpose of this examination is to build an understanding of the ethics of managing precarious academics from the perspective of NTRs and to explore how this model of 'ethical leadership' could provide insight into the rights and responsibilities of the institution for supporting their work. While we have interviewed a number of managers for the larger project, this paper examines the impact of managerial relationships for NTRs. We recognise, however, that many of the issues we highlight regarding institutional norms, discourses and practices are shared by academics regardless of their employment conditions.

## Managerial relationships and the academic precariat

The rise in casual employment and decreased availability of permanent contracts is an international trend (Acker and Haque 2017). In Australia, for example, those in precarious employment constitute up to 60% of the total workforce and up to 80% of research-only positions in some universities (Spina et al. 2020). The precarious positioning of much of the academic workforce highlights the need for improved structures and processes to better support and develop all academic staff. Percy et al. (2008) argue that sessional teaching staff make substantial contributions to their institutions, yet there is a lack of 'evidence of systemic sustainable policy and practice' (2) to support their employment, induction, management, career and professional development, and reward and recognition. They note the crucial role that management of sessional teachers plays in 'establishing quality processes in teaching and learning' (Percy et al. 2008, 13). Our research has identified that managers of NTRs play a similarly crucial role (Spina et al. 2020) and that all forms of managerial relationships, whether they are transactional relationships that occur solely through email or distanced communication or close collaborations, have an impact on the experiences of NTRs. Nonetheless, there is a dearth of research into the relations between NTRs and their managers, the practices of managers and how their roles might be developed, supported and formalised.

Regardless of whether tenured academics are overseeing teaching or research (or a combination of both), the quality of managerial relationships can contribute greatly to what Archer, Pajo, and Lee (2013, 14) term the 'broader employment relationship', which includes 'work flexibility, hours of work allocated, income level, certainty of work, facilities provided, and inclusion in social and communication networks'. In turn, these employment conditions have a significant impact on levels of job satisfaction, stress and future career opportunities for precarious employees. The consequences of precarity for NTRs in what has been called 'the gig academy' (Kezar, DePaola, and Scott 2019) have been well researched, from the identity work of 'coping' (Nikunen 2012), to financial insecurities, and mental health implications (ILO 2019; Spina et al. 2020). Insecurity of employment in conjunction with the pressure to engage in visible markers of scholarly productivity such as publishing can impact family life, relationships and even restrict possibilities of female academics (in particular) to have children (Rudick and Dannels 2019).

Managers of NTRs are generally tenured academic staff, who often receive little training for the role of management (Deem et al. 2000; Ryan, Connell, and Burgess 2017). It is important to not only understand NTRs' subjective experiences of precarity, but also how these experiences are being navigated and shaped by those who manage their work. The relationships between NTRs and their managers can highlight existing inequities in working conditions and experiences of working in a university. Building an understanding of these relationships can shine a light on the significant role that managers and forms of management can play for NTRs (Ryan, Connell, and Burgess 2017).

Despite the limited research on NTR management in universities, existing literature provides some insights into factors for developing these roles. Collinson (2004), for example, has examined occupational identities of contract researchers across different contexts in the UK. She notes important differences between small academic departments and large research teams in terms of researchers' opportunities for peer-to-peer learning and support. This research cites positive examples of informal peer mentoring and development in those departments or centres in which there are a critical mass of temporary researchers, and in contrast notes the sense of isolation and outsider status of those lacking peer contact. The present study raises key questions regarding the role that research managers play in providing support and building the capacity of the NTRs in their employ.

Nikunen (2012) observes that 'social support is important in an academic career, even though individualistic thinking and the notion of meritocracy tends to make this invisible to some degree' (276). The 'radical responsibilisation' (Fleming 2017) of the academic workforce positions individuals as responsible for their own work and the management, support and training of others. This relationship, however, is mediated by university demands, with all academics and employees in the academy constrained by institutional structures and processes. Decisions on recruitment, employment entitlements, length of contract, pay-scales and so on are framed by these boundaries. Academics in ongoing employment are subject to highly regulated demands of how their own work is managed and how they are able to manage the work of others, particularly those employed on 'soft money' (Kaplan 2010). Despite a need to navigate institutional processes and systems for managing NTRs, academics are rarely provided with any guidance in recruitment or management.

Tilbury (2008) offers a critical assessment of these managerial relationships, noting the 'ambivalence' of academics and Chief Investigators (CIs) on funded research projects 'at being forced into being "managers" of research projects' (3). This stance does not presuppose that academics will provide unfair or ineffective management. Rather, she suggests that many academics find themselves in managerial roles without any prior aspiration to manage people. While her main focus is 'the position of the hired underlings employed to undertake the research' (Tilbury 2008, 3), her work identifies challenges for academics and funding bodies to ensure that ethical work practices and support for NTRs are implemented. Tilbury (2008) identifies an absence of mechanisms within funding bodies to monitor actual, ongoing participation and commitment and suggests a need for these funders to monitor the management of research staff. Tilbury (2008) concludes that there is 'the need for CIs to develop a sympathetic and aware stance to the difficulties CRs [contract researchers] face, and a willingness to attempt to address these' (9), also noting that this will depend on a far more systematic and rigorous examination of prevailing institutional academic practices than is currently evident. In this paper, we argue a need for greater understanding of the practices of academics involved in the complex managerial work of overseeing research and researchers and associated ethical responsibilities in support of those they employ.

## Methods

Drawn from a larger data set of interviews with contract researchers and research managers in the UK and Australia (Spina et al. 2020), this paper analyses the in-depth accounts of 22 NTRs as they revealed the nature and importance of social relations between themselves and their managers. Participants were recruited via a snowball sampling technique, involving a general call for interest through Twitter and the researchers' academic networks. Due to the nature of the recruitment, some participants were previously known to the researchers, while others volunteered from a broad range of institutions across Australia and the UK. Semi-structured interviews with participants were conducted by the researchers either face-to-face or via video-conferencing with a duration of between 45 and 90 minutes. The participants worked at a range of institutions, predominantly universities, although some also worked in hospital research and research institutes. Descriptions of the participants' ages, time on contract and work environments has been provided (see Appendix). As part of the deidentification of participants, the specific institutions in which they worked have not been named. There was a diversity of employment for the participants, many worked across institutions in various roles and according to different employment conditions, including casual hours-based contracts, sessional teaching, and/ or fixed term positions (both part-time and full-time).

Our interviews, method of inquiry and analytic approach draw on the theoretical contributions of the critical feminist sociologist Dorothy E. Smith (1987). Smith's theoretical approach is based on an understanding that objectified forms of knowing formed from the standpoint of those in positions of authority are different from the knowing that is only possible through lived experience. This view encourages research inquiries to start with 'the actualities' of people's lives (Smith 2005, 31) and position individuals as 'active and competent knowers' (Smith 1987, 142). Following Smith (2005), we saw our discussion with participants as an opportunity to check our understandings, so as to locate their standpoints; making this the entry into our research. We acknowledge that as authors, we were both insiders and outsiders to the research. While we (the authors) have all worked in insecure positions in academia, two of us (Harris, Spina) are now employed in permanent academic positions as researchers and managers, two are working on fixed-term contracts (Bailey, Goff) and one is on a casual contract (Smithers). As such, we are both insiders and outsiders to the research. Griffith (1998), who worked extensively with Smith in the development of institutional ethnography, has described how a binary insider/outsider dichotomy lacks complexity, and that rather, 'the reflexive character of social inquiry' is critical because as researchers we are always 'both insiders and outsiders to the stories we explore' (362). In talking with participants and analysing our data, it was therefore important that we adopted a reflexive approach, engaging in frequent conversations as a team in which we shared our perspectives as employees in different states, countries and modes of employment. We have sought to reflect on the descriptions offered by participants, without making *a priori* judgements about social and power relations.

Smith's approach to understanding the coordination of the everyday is through an exploration of how texts are taken up, or activated, in local sites. Smith has written extensively (e.g. 1990, 2005) about the role of texts in modern societies and institutions, explaining how their use authorises particular courses of action, and mediates practices and social relations. As Campbell and Gregor (2002) explain, the capacity of a text to rule depends on how it 'carries messages across sites' (613), engaging readers and sparking activity. Our analytic approach affords an opportunity to bring to light the invisible work, issues and realities to which privileged groups (in this case, tenured academics and managers) – whose perspectives are embedded within dominant discourses and institutional practices – may otherwise be oblivious.

In addition to the use of Smith's sociological theoretical contributions, we draw on Starratt's (1991) tripartite model of ethical leadership to investigate the approaches adopted by managers of contract researchers. Ethical leadership is defined as a social, relational process whereby leaders treat their colleagues and employees fairly and justly (Ehrich et al. 2015). While primarily applied in studies of school leadership, Starratt's (1991, 1996) framework offers a useful heuristic for the exploration of ethical leadership for this study of the role of academic leaders and non-tenured researchers. The model describes three key ethics: an ethic of care, an ethic of justice and an ethic of critique. The ethic of care encourages leaders to be open to all voices and value the diverse opinions, relationships and ideas that occur within a workplace. The ethic of justice is 'understood as individual choices to act justly, and justice understood as the community's choice to direct or govern its actions justly' (Starratt 1996, 163). This ethic focuses on concepts of fairness and legality. The ethic of critique challenges leaders to reflect on the institutions and cultures in which they work in order to identify and redress issues of inequity or exploitation. While described and explored separately in this paper, these three ethics are inextricably linked and work to enhance one another by establishing a focus on fairness (justice), relationships (care) and disruption of the *status quo* (critique) (Starratt 1991, 1996).

Data analysis involved thematic coding of rich descriptions of interactions between NTRs and managers. We first identified instances where NTRs described their relationships with managers and examples of practices the managers were described to undertake. Following Smith, we made use of the rich descriptions of embodied experiences described by our participants in our analysis, considering the commonalities associated with the management of NTRs in academia as a systemic concern that is evident in multiple sites. In analysing our data, we have looked to understand the actualities of work for people, without making *a priori* judgements of how social and power relations come to be as they are; this included identifying the 'texts' which are activated in the everyday practices of NTRs. We made use of Starratt's tripartite model of ethical leadership to thematically code the rich descriptions into three categories: ethic of justice, ethic of care and ethic of critique.

Our analysis of interviews with NTRs highlighted practices aligning with Starratt's (1991, 1996) model of ethical leadership. The most frequently cited practices included management behaviours focused on creating a fair and equitable work environment, such as those linked with Starratt's ethic of justice. Examples of managers engaging in critiques of dominant discourses and systemic boundaries that shape the experiences of NTRs, however, were rarely offered. Our analysis examines the texts which managers in higher education have to guide them and explores how the texts that are activated become less transparent and accessible as we consider different elements of the ethical leadership framework.

## The everyday experiences of non-tenured researchers negotiating (un-)ethical leadership

The NTRs interviewed reported a wide variety of social relationships and experiences that were highly influential in their work and lives. A common thread throughout these interviews, however, was the role of their managers, typically lead researchers of the projects on which they were employed. Given the 'relative paucity' (Deem 2006) of training for managers, it is unsurprising that NTRs' experiences of management were characterised by diversity, even within the same institutions. Starting with the everyday experiences of these NTRs, our analysis highlighted a hierarchy of ethical leadership practices as we uncovered their accounts of the institutional texts activated by their managers (Smith 1987).

## *Ethic of justice*

Managers are often focussed on attending to mandatory conditions of employment as inscribed in key texts such as labour laws and institutional policies. Employment processes provide a form of 'textually-mediated social interaction' (Campbell and Gregor 2002, 29), whereby texts such as national legal requirements and employment contracts transform the actualities of employment into 'standardised, generalised, and, especially translocal forms of coordinating people's activities' (Smith 2005, 101). In institutional ethnographic terms, local employment of contract researchers is orchestrated by a range of texts that coordinate the actions and practices of managers across multiple sites, creating a regime of institutional governance.

Starratt (1991, 1996) argued that an ethic of justice is built on democratic principles and the concept of 'fairness'. The NTRs who we interviewed indicated their managers adhered to this principle of 'fairness' through institutional process-driven, textually mediated (Smith 2005) practices including ensuring contracts were signed and processed, timesheets were approved, staff logins were acquired, and so on. Given the financial insecurity experienced by many contract researchers, these processes were critical in their experience of employment (Broadbent and Strachan 2016).

The unstructured nature of insecure academic work means there are few textually authorised requirements in comparison to the formal protections afforded to tenured academics. The lack of textual protection means that when managers do not exhibit an ethic of justice, NTRs are particularly vulnerable. Jill illustrates this:

> [On a 12-month contract] you get paid for those holidays and Christmas, and you get 17 and a half percent super[1]! But now, he's cottoned on to that, so [my manager would] only give me 11-month contracts. I finish on the 19th of December and come back at the end of January. The thing is he thinks that, 'Oh, well, we're gonna be closed then.'

Jill's manager reduced her contract term without considering how this period of unemployment would affect Jill. Jill's experience demonstrates one way in which neoliberal industrial policies have enabled budgets to become prioritised ahead of people. It is possible that this decision was taken by the manager with a view to meeting budgetary goals; being ethical in respect to the use of public funding for research. It is further possible that this manager is not aware that this break in employment could have significant financial implications for Jill, where for most academics in ongoing positions, this time could be taken as paid leave. While it may not be legally problematic to use contracts that are shorter than 12 months, it is a questionable practice in terms of the ethic of justice.

The lack of institutional guidance or policies around employment practices means that the experiences of NTRs may be invisible to managing academics. For instance, Amelia explained a situation where an academic who had employed her on an hourly paid contract during the year,

> [they] said, 'I'm away now and I'm taking time off, so I'm not going to need you till the end of next February,' and I was going, 'Well, that's just fantastic … three months off … ' You know … there's probably nobody nicer than her to work with … she's just gorgeous, you know?

While Amelia described a strong positive working relationship with her manager, which she wished to continue, she explained that she was left without any paid employment during this period of leave. Academics managing research projects may be oriented towards the textual demands of their own projects, including managing budgets and performance indicators. In this way, institutional texts, including fixed-term and casual contracts and the performance expectations of permanently employed academics, textually mediate the work and everyday lives of all academics, including NTRs. These targets, however, are unlikely to include any expectations around the management of research staff (Tilbury 2008). Managers who engaged with the embodied experiences of contract researchers, and adopted an ethic of justice (often in small ways) were frequently praised by NTRs, like Jill who reported:

> I know it's only two days a week, but always the contract came ... [the] renewal came well in advance of the other one expiring.

Jill was not alone in expressing her appreciation for managers who ensured that employment contracts were in place before work commenced or before the current contract ended. In contrast, our participants also reported that practices such as reducing hours and scheduling contracts around project demands were common. Many indicated that they did not receive employment contracts until they had completed a substantial proportion of their work hours. The reports of NTRs suggest a worrying trend where minimum compliance with employment relations and conditions is seen to represent a relatively high standard of management. The situated realities of their employment and lives beyond were often invisible even, as Amelia described it, to 'nice' and 'gorgeous' managers.

Some of the participants outlined situations where they felt there had been a lack of justice in terms of recognising their contributions to research. An ethic of justice includes fairness in ensuring that opportunities and resources, such as opportunities for future employment through meeting institutional requirements or authoring papers are provided (Starratt 1996). Being named on papers that they had co-authored was considered surprising by some of the interviewed NTRs, as they expressed that it was not always the case to be named when they had contributed to writing. When offered, the attribution of authorship, however, could raise other issues in terms of the order in which co-authors of publications were acknowledged. Some NTRs provided examples where lead authorship was given to more senior tenured academics, some of whom had not provided substantial contribution to writing or the intellectual development of publications. Riley said:

> I only get a bit cross in the authorship stakes if ... others are listed as authors and they've made no substantial contribution whatsoever ... They're listed before me and I'm listed like last when I've done most of the work. That really annoys me.

Similarly, Emma said that research she conducted for a manager was later used for a successful grant application, 'that I didn't get a job on'. Laura described a lack of transparency in hiring practices at her research centre, saying that new jobs that are advertised and filled externally 'are a surprise to us every single time'.

Later in the interview, Laura described an instance where she refused to collect data without first obtaining consent from her research participants, while a colleague decided to remain quiet and follow the directions of the manager. Laura said:

EDUCATIONAL LEADERSHIP AND POLICY IN A TIME OF PRECARITY    45

[My colleague] was the one who got her name put on; who got invited to participate on those publications and ongoing work with [the manager]. So she's getting … it's almost like a promotion, while I get shut out. And part of me thinks, well fine, because I don't want to work with someone who's unethical; but it's cost me.

At the 'tenuous periphery' (Kimber 2003), NTRs are placed in unequal power relationships where they feel they have very little choice but to conform to the dominant institutional norms. Opaque and informal hiring practices and the use of NTRs' intellectual contributions to further the careers of others were just some examples that illustrate the culturally normative behaviour of academia in which NTRs felt they had little option but to allow these practices to continue.

With an ethic of justice understood as 'individual choices to act justly' (Starratt 1991, 163), the above extracts provide illustrations of some behaviours that may be considered (un)just. With a system built on networking as a means for gaining further work (Spina et al. 2020), like Laura, NTRs often felt they had to choose boundaries for what they perceived to be questionable practices of their managers. While there are established guidelines for determining authorship, our interview data suggests that these texts might not always be followed or considered by the managers of NTRs. In comparison to regulatory texts such as employment laws, texts like the Vancouver Convention (http://www.icmje.org/icmje-recommendations.pdf) were not invoked. Given that there is little oversight of those who manage NTRs, this finding is concerning and suggests that institutional attention to such conventions might be useful for those in management positions.

### *Ethic of care*

An ethic of care is built on a belief in human dignity that 'requires fidelity to persons, a willingness to acknowledge their right to be who they are, an openness to encountering them in their authentic individuality, a loyalty to relationship' (Starratt 1996, 163). Social relations are at the heart of care ethics, guiding practice and shaping everyday realities. While we do not suggest that it is the case for all managerial relationships, our research found many examples among our participants where strong, caring relationships had been established between managers and NTRs.

Often care-related practices led to important outcomes that changed the subjectivities, everyday realities and trajectories of contract researchers. These practices can be described broadly as 'capacity-building', comprising three main elements: building the skills and publications of NTRs, networking, and mentoring. For instance, Stacey said:

Actually [my manager] has been quite a mentoring role, she has been very supportive and, kind of I guess, helping me to build connections as well that she thought might lead towards other grants. I think she's been basically supportive.

Collaboration on grants or research papers were important for NTRs, and typically only accessible when their managers afforded opportunities for them to be (and feel) part of a research community. Opportunities for co-authorship, professional development and grants were highly valued, although when these occurred, they were often accompanied by a sense of surprise. One possible explanation for this sense of surprise is that institutional policies and processes do not require academic managers to undertake supportive, mentoring roles. The time pressure experienced by many academics, both in ongoing and precarious employment, means that the level of support offered by these managers are viewed as generously going beyond the required managerial relationships in ways that are not always recognised or rewarded by the institution.

Caring managers were often described as those who took opportunities to talk to NTRs to learn about their career goals and research interests. These managers often provided opportunities for contract researchers to extend their knowledge or build their resume. To illustrate, we draw on Sandra's experience:

> They're so generous with their knowledge and their time, so when I applied for some funding to do my own project, they were really supportive of that and gave me lots of advice. Really, really nice because they're really busy people but they always make time for that, which is lovely, I think.

This support is characterised by Sandra as the generosity and care of individual managers. Her response supports the notion that the provision of time, knowledge and advice is not viewed as a necessary component of the managerial role. Rather, spending time to develop the capacity of a more junior researcher in precarious employment is considered an unexpected positive attribute of the individuals involved, who are referred to as 'generous' and 'supportive'. This discourse was common across our dataset and suggests that activities grounded in an ethic of care – i.e. sharing of knowledge and resources, an interest in researchers' trajectories and so forth – was important but could not be taken-for-granted. Managers demonstrating an ethic of care was viewed as an individual act of generosity and kindness.

The lack of this ethic of care between managers and contract researchers left many feeling unsupported and vulnerable. For example, some researchers experienced far more distant relationships with their academic managers, which resulted in them being left without clear instructions about institutional policies or even what work they should be doing. Felix said:

> I keep getting emails from HR asking me about putting together things with my supervisor. I'm like, 'I can't, I don't know … ' Someone said to me at the end of last week, 'So what have they got you doing?' I'm like, 'Who's 'they'? What do you mean?'. No one's really come and spoken to me yet.

Rachel similarly described a project led by a manager as toxic, saying that some days she felt:

> I'd probably rather jump in front of a bus than get on it to come to work. Terrible. It's horrible. I can remember catching the bus to work some days thinking, 'Gee, I wish we'd crash'.

These experiences were not only isolating, they were also reflective of the modern neoliberal university in which individualisation has become commonplace, and social relations are organised by textually mediated institutional expectations. Any management practice that has a collective focus is considered to be 'above and beyond' (Rawlins, Hansen, and Jorgensen 2011).

Dominant discourses in the neoliberal university comprise notions of individualisation and competition (Hey 2001). Within these discourses, NTRs are positioned as the 'other', who must engage in competition and adopt the risks of precarious employment. Perhaps reflective of individualising policies, reports of 'backstabbing' were common, including practices that used NTRs' work to advance one's own career with limited or no acknowledgement. Managers who worked against these ideals of individualisation and acted with an ethic of care were considered to be doing so outside of institutional norms. This is reflective, perhaps, of the lack of guiding texts which managers can 'activate' to undertake in management roles. Texts that managers can access are usually focused on employment practices, such as employment laws, rather than on social relations which are at the basis of an ethic of care.

### *Ethic of critique*

An ethic of critique involves an understanding of power relations within dominant discourses and how these privilege certain groups and create groups of 'others'. In practice, an ethic of critique means managers speaking out against unfair policies which create exclusionary practices for NTRs. Our research suggests that despite the precarity faced by NTRs, their managers did not often seek to mitigate risks for them. As this research has examined the perspectives of NTRs, we cannot say that managers did not undertake activism in ways that were not observed by those in their employ. The overwhelming majority of NTRs in this research, however, reported that they had not experienced managers engaging in activism to improve the employment conditions of precariously employed workers. We recognise that both tenured and non-tenured staff are subject to power relations in universities and it can be difficult for managers to find effective ways of pushing back against the prevailing discourses within their institution's policies and practices.

One systemic issue discussed by NTRs was specific rules regarding who could and could not be assigned a lead role, or at times a role at all, on a funded project. For example,

> [There was] a grant bid which was bigger and I put a lot more work into it [than others on the team]. [When we got the grant], I tried to be the PI [Principal Investigator] for it, and I was told I wasn't allowed to. I was only allowed to be a co-invesitgator. And then it went from bad to worse, my time got reduced on it because all the permanent people on the bid – nine out of ten – there's a way of costing them. Because my time's fixed I was becoming too expensive, so my time got reduced massively so I'm doing the least out of everyone (Neil)

In this scenario, translocal policies prevented Neil from being named as lead investigator on the project, despite Neil providing a large contribution to the formation of the grant. In another example, Emma was excluded from a funded project due to the budget not being sufficient to accommodate NTRs who hold a PhD:

> It was actually quite annoying ... when your supervisor gets an ARC [Australian Research Council grant] that is roughly in your area, you are like, 'YES!' Then they ended up with not enough money to employ people with PhD's! So all the research work went to people who had not yet finished the PhD. Which was really like 'Oh! Ugh!' Very annoying.

Invoking Smith (2005), we see that the guiding text for managers in this scenario is the allocated research personnel budget. This text is central to the regulation of fixed-term and casual research employment contracts. An ethic of critique 'reveals that the organisation in its present forms is a source of unethical consequences' (Starratt 1991, 190).

Industrial agreements typically specify a higher pay scale for contract researchers who have completed a PhD. In this case, Emma was not hired due to the extra cost associated with her qualification. Her example illustrates the authority of budgets as a key institutional text that mediate and coordinate social relations (Smith 2005). This process also signifies the current limits of the management of researchers, which make it possible for tenured academics to make *ad hoc* decisions regarding their own projects, without *having to* consider the impacts of this upon the NTRs they employ. There is limited guidance available for managers, who seek to challenge dominant discourses of NTRs as 'other' or 'disposable commodities' and support the ongoing employment and capacity building of academics. We did not encounter any examples in our interview data describing managers practising in an ethic of critique. This is not to say that managers *didn't* engage in practices critical of university employment policies. If this occurred, however, their practices did not feature strongly in the experiences described by NTRs.

## Discussion

Researchers who secure funding and lecturers teaching large courses frequently seek support from those employed on a contract basis. Many find themselves with responsibilities to manage NTRs and sessional staff without prior experience (Percy et al. 2008) or any prior aspiration to engage in management practices (Tilbury 2008). While managers play a critical role in shaping the experiences of those they employ, the literature reports they are provided with limited training (Nadolny and Ryan 2015; Qualter and Willis 2012). There is wide variation across faculties and institutions, however, training is often limited to statutory or practical requirements, including anti-discrimination legislation or managing pay claims (Baik, Naylor, and Corrin 2018).

Descriptions of everyday experiences of ethical leadership of NTRs are characterised by a diverse and sometimes unsettling set of management practices. Many interviewees within this study ascribed unethical behaviour by their managers to culturally normative behaviour, as the 'way things are done' within the institution. In contrast, the ethical leadership practices of some managers were praised and they were considered 'good' managers – yet the benchmark against which managerial conduct was judged in these cases was often very low. The limitations of training and support for managers and the activation of specific institutional texts, including policies and processes, offer some rationale for the differing characterisations of management practices. Our interview extracts provide an illustration of ethical, supportive management practices within academia that are 'notable' in the descriptions of the everyday experiences of NTRs.

Within the neoliberal university context, minimum requirements unsurprisingly define the expectations for some managers. The application of Smith's sociological approach to interviews for this study has highlighted how textually based practices mediate and shape the ethical practices of managers. Aspects of ethical leadership, particularly in terms of the ethic of justice, are driven by 'boss texts' that authorise particular actions by managers. These 'boss texts' are largely related to employment practices and are mediated by texts such as anti-discrimination legislation, employment contracts and salary scales. The majority of ethical practices described in these interviews can be characterised as aligning with the ethic of justice, in which employment principles around just and equitable treatment are applied to the management of NTRs. This is not to say that we did not hear multiple stories in which precariously employed academics had been subject to unjust treatment, for instance, not being paid on time, or not having signed employment contracts.

Imbued in the talk of the contract researchers was the reality that tenured academics' work is increasingly organised through a focus on achieving specific key performance indicators or targets. The focus on such texts coordinates relations between tenured and non-tenured academics. Working under managers who have not adopted an ethic of care in managing these relations typically meant NTRs found themselves in a vulnerable position as they sought to build the academic capital needed to maintain continuous employment. However, as described above, there were instances in which tenured academics had adopted an ethical stance in which they attended to both the short and long term needs of NTRs. While relations of rule were focussed on meeting KPIs, individuals used their agency to work outside of textual realities, for instance by offering co-authorship opportunities, advocating for ongoing employment, funding professional development and so on. This work is likely to be invisible to universities, as it is not evident in textually produced versions of how academic work is constituted. As a result, the NTRs interviewed as part of this study who experienced managers that engaged in practices aligned with the ethic of care generally ascribed these behaviours to individual generosity and kindness.

Finally, we found little evidence of an ethic of critique where tenured academics might challenge dominant discourses and institutional structures that negatively impact the careers of NTRs. We suggest that while tenured academics may feel prepared to operate outside of textually mediated relations to undertake caring work on an individual basis, they may not feel that they are in a position to question existing structures and ruling relations. Indeed, many tenured academics may have lived through significant periods of unstable employment themselves, and therefore be highly aware of the dangers of precarity. Remaining silent about policies and discourses that disadvantage and exclude NTRs may be a means of safeguarding their own employment in unstable times. While 'caring for' NTRs can be undertaken informally by managers, formal acknowledgement of institutional structures that limit their ability to engage in the ethic of care is required to disrupt dominant discourses and engage with the ethic of critique. This individualisation of risk and responsibility is precisely the outcome to which neoliberal regimes are oriented.

The relationship between managers and NTRs is a crucial point of focus because of the increasing divide between the tenured 'core' and the precarious 'periphery' (Kimber 2003). This divide is operationalised by a split labour market in which the core is recruited and employed in respect to formal standards, while the periphery must learn to negotiate a variety of informal means to gain and maintain employment. Furthermore, the informal nature of the casual job market means that administrators and core academics can make hire and fire decisions for which there are no formal obligations regarding the inclusion of the peripheral academic. For these reasons, Mauri (2019, 186) refers to core academics as 'proxy-employers' upon whom the 'reserve army' of casual labour depend for employment. This position of mediation between informal and formal economies invests core academics with great power. Just as employers have a duty of care to their employees, core academics have a duty of care to their casual staff. Yet in the relative absence of formal standards and texts according to which such a duty might be discharged, this becomes a matter of ethics.

## Note

1. 'Super' refers to superannuation. Superannuation in Australia refers to the system where employees and employers set aside money that accumulates and funds retirement.

## Disclosure statement

No potential conflict of interest was reported by the author(s).

## ORCID

*Kathleen Smithers* ⓘ http://orcid.org/0000-0001-7301-5658
*Jess Harris* ⓘ http://orcid.org/0000-0003-4584-6993
*Mhorag Goff* ⓘ http://orcid.org/0000-0003-4936-2881
*Nerida Spina* ⓘ http://orcid.org/0000-0002-2923-0104
*Simon Bailey* ⓘ http://orcid.org/0000-0001-9142-2791

## References

Acker, Sandra, and Eve Haque. 2017. "Left Out in the Academic Field: Doctoral Graduates Deal with a Decade of Disappearing Jobs." *Canadian Journal of Higher Education/Revue canadienne d'enseignement supérieur* 47 (3): 101–119.

Archer, John, Karl Pajo, and Louise Lee. 2013. "Perceptions of Precariousness and Employment Strain: The Role of the Manager." Paper presented at the annual meeting for Australia and New Zealand Academy of Management, Hobart, December 4–6.

Baik, Chi, Ryan Naylor, and Linda Corrin. 2018. "Developing a Framework for University-Wide Improvement in Training and Support of 'Casual' Academics." *Journal of Higher Education Policy and Management* 40 (4): 375–389. doi:10.1080/1360080X.2018.1479948.

Brady, Malcom, and Anthony Briody. 2016. "Strategic Use of Temporary Employment Contracts as Real Options." *Journal of General Management* 42 (2): 31–56.

Broadbent, Kaye, and Glenda Strachan. 2016. "'It's Difficult to Forecast Your Longer Term Career Milestone': Career Development and Insecure Employment for Research Academics in Australian Universities." *Labour & Industry: A Journal of the Social and Economic Relations of Work* 26 (4): 251–265. doi:10.1080/10301763.2016.1243438.

Campbell, Marie, and Frances Gregor. 2002. *Mapping Social Relations: A Primer in Doing Institutional Ethnography.* Lanham: AltaMira Press.

Collinson, J. A. 2004. "Occupational Identity on the Edge: Social Science Contract Researchers in Higher Education." *Sociology* 38 (2): 313–329. doi:10.1177/0038038504040866.

Deem, Rosemary. 2006. "Changing Research Perspectives on the Management of Higher Education: Can Research Permeate the Activities of Manager-Academics?" *Higher Education Quarterly* 60 (3): 203–228.

Deem, Rosemary, Oliver Fulton, Sam Hillyard, Rachel Johnson, and Mike Reed. 2000. "Managing Contemporary UK Universities – Manager-Academics and New Managerialism." *Academic Leadership-Online Journal* 1 (3).

Ehrich, Lisa C., Jessica Harris, Val Klenowski, Judy Smeed, and Nerida Spina. 2015. "The Centrality of Ethical Leadership." *Journal of Educational Administration* 53 (2): 197–214. doi:10.1108/JEA-10-2013-0110.

Fleming, Peter. 2017. "The Human Capital Hoax: Work, Debt and Insecurity in the Era of Uberization." *Organization Studies* 38 (5): 691–709.

Griffith, Alison I. 1998. "Insider/Outsider: Epistemological Privilege and Mothering Work." *Human Studies* 21 (4): 361–376. doi:10.1023/A:1005421211078.

Hey, Valerie. 2001. "The Construction of Academic Time: sub/Contracting Academic Labour in Research." *Journal of Education Policy* 16 (1): 67–84. doi:10.1080/02680930010009831.

Holmwood, John, and Chaime Marcuello Servós. 2019. "Challenges to Public Universities: Digitalisation, Commodification and Precarity." *Social Epistemology* 33 (4): 309–320.

ILO. 2019. *Final Report, Global Dialogue Forum on Employment Terms and Conditions in Tertiary Education.* Geneva: International Labour Office.

Kaplan, Karen. 2010. "Academia: The Changing Face of Tenure." *Nature* 468 (7320): 123–125.

Kezar, Adrianna, Tom DePaola, and Daniel T. Scott. 2019. *The Gig Academy: Mapping Labor in the Neoliberal University.* Baltimore: Johns Hopkins University Press.

Kimber, Megan. 2003. "The Tenured 'Core' and the Tenuous 'Periphery': The Casualisation of Academic Work in Australian Universities." *Journal of Higher Education Policy and Management* 25 (1): 41–50. doi:10.1080/13600800305738.

Lewchuk, Wayne, Alice De Wolff, Andy King, and Michael Polanyi. 2003. "From job Strain to Employment Strain: Health Effects of Precarious Employment." *Just Labour* 3: 23–35.

Macfarlane, Bruce. 2011. "The Morphing of Academic Practice: Unbundling and the Rise of the Para-Academic." *Higher Education Quarterly* 65 (1): 59–73.

Mauri, Christian. 2019. "Formulating the Academic Precariat." In *The Social Structures of Global Academia*, edited by Fabian Cannizzo and Nick Osbaldiston. London: Routledge

Nadolny, Anthony, and Suzanne Ryan. 2015. "McUniversities Revisited: A Comparison of University and McDonald's Casual Employee Experiences in Australia." *Studies in Higher Education* 40 (1): 142–157. doi:10.1080/03075079.2013.818642.

Nikunen, Minna. 2012. "Precarious Work at the 'Entrepreneurial' University: Adaptation Versus 'Abandon Ship' Individualization and Identity Work: Coping with the 'Entrepreneurial' University." In *Higher Education Research in Finland. Emerging Structures and Contemporary*

*Issues*, edited by Sakari Ahola and D. M. Hoffman, 271–290. Jyväskylä: Jyväskylä University Press.

Percy, Alisa, Michele Scoufis, Sharron Parry, Allan Goody, Margaret Hicks, Ian Macdonald, Kay Martinez, et al. 2008. *The RED Report, Recognition – Enhancement – Development: The Contribution of Sessional Teachers to Higher Education*. Sydney: Australian Learning and Teaching Council.

Qualter, Anne, and Ian Willis. 2012. "Protecting Academic Freedom in Changing Times: The Role of Heads of Departments." *Journal of Educational Administration and History* 44 (2): 121–139. doi:10.1080/00220620.2012.658765.

Rawlins, Peter, Sally Hansen, and Lone Jorgensen. 2011. "Immigrant or Refugee: Perceived Effects of Colonisation of Academia by Market Forces." *Journal of Educational Administration and History* 43 (2): 165–179. doi:10.1080/00220620.2011.560254.

Rudick, C. K., and D. P. Dannels. 2019. "'Yes, and …' Continuing the Scholarly Conversation About Contingent Labor in Higher Education." *Communication Education* 68 (2): 259–263.

Ryan, Suzanne, Julia Connell, and John Burgess. 2017. "Casual Academics: A new Public Management Paradox." *Labour & Industry: a Journal of the Social and Economic Relations of Work* 27 (1): 56–72.

Slaughter, Sheila, and Gary Rhoades. 2004. *Academic Capitalism and the New Economy: Markets, State, and Higher Education*. Baltimore: John Hopkins University Press.

Smith, Dorothy E. 1987. *The Everyday World as Problematic: A Feminist Sociology*. Toronto: University of Toronto Press.

Smith, Dorothy E. 1990. *Texts, Facts and Femininity: Exploring the Relations of Ruling*. London: Routledge.

Smith, Dorothy E. 2005. *Institutional Ethnography: A Sociology for People*. Oxford: Rowman AltaMira Press.

Spina, Nerida, Jess Harris, Simon Bailey, and Mhorag Goff. 2020. *'Making it' as a Contract Researcher: A Pragmatic Look at Precarious Work*. Abingdon: Routledge.

Starratt, R. J. 1991. "Building an Ethical School: A Theory for Practice in Educational Leadership." *Educational Administration Quarterly* 27 (2): 185–202.

Starratt, R. J. 1996. *Transforming Educational Administration: Meaning, Community and Excellence*. New York: McGraw Hill.

Stringer, Rebecca, Dianne Smith, Rachel Spronken-Smith, and Cheryl Wilson. 2018. "'My Entire Career Has Been Fixed Term': Gender and Precarious Academic Employment at a New Zealand University." *New Zealand Sociology* 33 (2): 196–201.

Tilbury, Fiona. 2008. "'Piggy in the Middle': The Liminality of the Contract Researcher in Funded 'Collaborative' Research." *Sociological Research Online* 12 (6): 32–43.

Winter, Richard. 2009. "Academic Manager or Managed Academic? Academic Identity Schisms in Higher Education." *Journal of Higher Education Policy and Management* 31 (2): 121–131.

## Appendix

| Name | Age (approx.) | Countries | Institutions worked for | Length of time in research |
|---|---|---|---|---|
| Amelia | 40s | Australia and New Zealand | Universities; research institutes | 10+ |
| Amy | 40s | Australia and United States of America | Universities; think tanks | 10+ |
| Ashley | 20s | Australia | Universities | 5–10 |
| Billie | 30s | Australia and United States of America | Universities | 5–10 |
| Blake | 20s | Australia | Universities; research institutes | 0–5 |
| Stacey | 30s | United Kingdom | Universities | 0–5 |
| Charles | 50s | Australia | Universities; community organisations | 10+ |
| Chris | 40s | Australia | Universities; community groups | 5–10 |
| Elaine | 30s | Australia and United States of America | Universities | 10+ |
| Ethan | 30s | Australia | Universities; community organisations | 5–10 |
| Emma | 40s | Australia | Universities; community groups | 10+ |
| Jill | 50s | Australia | Universities; research institutes | 5–10 |
| Jordan | 30s | Australia | Universities; government research centre | 0–5 |
| Julia | 40s | United Kingdom | Universities | 10+ |
| Kathy | 30s | Australia and United States of America | Australian and American universities | 6–10 |
| Laura | 30s | Australia | Universities; government research centre | 10+ |
| Nell | 40s | United Kingdom | Universities | 10+ |
| Penny | 40s | New Zealand and Australia | Universities; research institutes | 10+ |
| Rachel | 30s | Australia | Universities; hospitals; research institutes | 10+ |
| Riley | 30s | Australia | Universities | 0–5 |
| Sandra | 30s | Australia and Canada | Universities; government research centre; hospitals | 5–10 |
| Sam | 30s | Australia | Universities | 5–10 |
| Felix | 50s | Australia | Universities | 0–5 |
| Taylor | 30s | United Kingdom | Universities | 0–5 |

# Teachers, fixed-term contracts and school leadership: toeing the line and jumping through hoops

Meghan Stacey [ID], Scott Fitzgerald [ID], Rachel Wilson [ID], Susan McGrath-Champ [ID] and Mihajla Gavin [ID]

**ABSTRACT**
Fixed-term contracts are a relatively recent, yet growing category of employment for teachers in the public school system in New South Wales (NSW), Australia. In this article, we draw on quantitative and qualitative data from a large state-wide survey ($N = 18,234$) of members of the public-school teacher union, the NSW Teachers' Federation, in order to explore the workload reports of teachers in temporary employment. We find that overall, these teachers report similar levels of workload to staff employed on a permanent basis. Experiences of work are, however, qualitatively different, with many in the temporary category feeling they must work harder than permanent teachers in order to 'prove themselves' to school executive. We argue that such experiences of precariousness may have particular 'scarring' effects for teachers in temporary employment, including gendered patterns of career progression, and discuss implications for leadership and policy.

## Introduction

Forms of precarious labour are increasing globally (Cuervo and Wyn 2016). In public schools in the Australian state of New South Wales (NSW), the category of fixed-term contract work known as 'temporary' teaching has been growing steadily over the past 20 years. In this article, we examine this new employment category in NSW public schools, as a feature of the employment landscape with hitherto largely undocumented implications for experiences of work and career progression. To do this, we present quantitative and qualitative data from a workload survey of 18,234 teachers, about one fifth of whom were in temporary employment, situating our examination of these data within a policy context of devolved authority in schools.

In what follows, we present the background of the current employment policy landscape for public school teachers in NSW. We then explore the literature on precarious work in school teaching and outline the conceptual framings drawn upon in this article. After describing our research methods, we present our findings, exploring the nature of work and workload for teachers in temporary employment and current tensions, as well as implications, for leadership in schools.

## Background

Teachers in NSW public schools work in one of three main employment categories – casual, temporary and permanent. The category of temporary teacher is the newest, established in 2001. Since then, while casual employment has remained relatively stable at 10%, the temporary category has grown to account for approximately 20% of the teacher workforce, while the proportion of permanent employment has declined from around 85% to 70% (McGrath-Champ et al. under review). The category of 'temporary' teacher in NSW was established as a new industrially-recognised employment type in response to growing concerns around casualisation and a need to ensure greater employment security for, in particular, women returning to the workforce after having children. In a legal case run by the NSW public sector teachers' union spanning 10 years and reaching the level of the High Court, an industrial settlement was reached between the state teachers' union and NSW Department of Education providing for the category of 'temporary' teacher, enshrining improved employment conditions and pay (for a more detailed analysis of the evolution of this employment category, see McGrath-Champ et al. under review). Historically, 'casual' teachers in NSW had their pay and conditions protected under a Casual Teachers Award, however a 'barrier' on the teachers' pay scale prevented casual teachers reaching higher pay levels, acting as a catalyst for the creation of the 'temporary' category (see McGrath-Champ et al. under review). While originating at least in part out of concern regarding casual conditions, these shifts reflect broader national and international trends over the past half-century, in which the conditions of traditionally 'stable' forms of employment, such as teaching, have eroded alongside the introduction of 'new public sector management' strategies associated with greater precarity of work (O'Sullivan et al. 2020).

Explorations of temporary teaching as a burgeoning employment category in NSW are therefore likely to have resonance with other forms of fixed-term contract teaching work around the globe. Australia overall, at 14%, would seem to have a lower proportion of teachers on fixed-term contracts when compared to the international average (18%) (Thomson and Hillman 2020) (although notably, this international average is similar to the proportion in the state of NSW [CESE 2018; McGrath-Champ et al. under review]). The Australian average is higher than in lower-secondary schools in England (6%), but lower than in the United States (33%) (OECD 2014). Types of fixed-term contract and casual employment in teaching are sometimes referred to in these contexts as 'supply' (UK) or 'substitute' (US) teaching (Charteris, Jenkins, Bannister-Tyrell, et al. 2017). In NSW, while a teacher employed in a casual capacity is 'employed on a day-to-day basis to meet relief needs within the school', a teacher employed in a temporary capacity is 'employed full-time for four weeks to a year, or part-time for two terms or more', receiving 'most of the entitlements of permanent teachers' (NSW Department of Education 2020), for instance including sick leave.

The creation and growth of the temporary employment category must also be understood in the context of devolved school governance. Along with enhanced flexibility and discretion around financial management afforded to local school principals (Gavin and

McGrath-Champ 2017), the 'Local Schools, Local Decisions' (LSLD) reform, progressively implemented from 2012 to 2020, increased principals' capacity for the selection of teaching staff. This policy shift enabled principals to make merit-based selection of one in two permanent staff appointments to their school, with the other half of staffing appointments filled by the central Department of Education. Meanwhile, all temporary positions are filled at school level, including – in particular circumstances, such as a projected decline in enrolments – the possible filling of a permanent position with a temporary appointment (NSW Government 2020). This policy context shaping NSW public schools has constituted a devolved employment settlement for Department employees, with greater decision-making regarding individuals' employment in the hands of local principal 'managers' rather than the state.

### *Temporary teaching in the research literature*

Research on fixed-term contract teaching work is a developing area of scholarship, with a distinct lack of research noted around the globe (e.g. for an analysis of the Canadian context, see The Alberta Teachers' Association 2011). Research in Australia has focused primarily on day-to-day casual work (Bamberry 2011; Charteris, Jenkins, Bannister-Tyrrell, et al. 2017; Charteris, Jenkins, Jones, et al. 2017; Jenkins, Smith, and Maxwell 2009; McCormack and Thomas 2005), unsurprising perhaps given that fixed-term work is rather 'newer'. When fixed-term contract employment is examined, it is often rolled together with other forms of precarious employment. In Bamberry's (2011) research, for instance, the temporary category is considered to be a particular kind of casual work, alongside the day-to-day casual.

However, the distinction between these employment types is important. McCormack and Thomas' (2005) research with casual teachers found that they preferred employment in blocks of time at one school, compared to day-to-day casual employment, as it allowed for more relationship-building, stronger integration into the systems and processes of individual schools, and overall a broader sense of skill building. Teachers on fixed-term contracts, meanwhile, were more likely to embed themselves in the school but did not feel they received the same sense of investment in return, not receiving access to training or updates about curriculum changes, for instance (Bamberry 2011). The literature on fixed-term contract teaching work has also noted a positive relationship between organisational citizenship behaviours (i.e. a person's voluntary effort and commitment) and perceived job insecurity, reflecting a desire to 'impress' management (Feather and Rauter 2004). There is, however, some evidence that this relationship may not be as strong in contexts where there is less competition for temporary teaching work (Lierich and O'Connor 2009).

Notwithstanding the importance of distinctions between temporary and casual forms of precariousness in teaching – a central issue to which this article contributes empirically – insights can nevertheless be drawn from the literature which explores the experience of day-to-day casual teaching. This research notes that, for instance, casual teachers describe a sense of feeling surveilled and needing to be 'deferential and grateful' in order to be asked back (Charteris et al. 2017, 520), often feeling marginalised and 'othered' within schools (Charteris, Jenkins, Bannister-Tyrrell, et al. 2017). While for some teachers a casual position might mean additional flexibility, for many, it also contributes to a life of day-to-day uncertainty, not knowing the facilities and routines of different schools and often failing to be provided with the information and resources necessary to do what is asked (Jenkins, Smith, and Maxwell 2009).

The experience of insecure casual and temporary work is particularly significant for those commencing their teaching careers. In NSW, it is today considered normal for teachers to begin their career in a casual or temporary capacity (NSW Department of Education 2020). Around Australia, only 22% of teachers in their first year are estimated by Preston (2019) to be in permanent positions, reflecting a substantial shift in the period between 2004 and 2013, with a decline in permanent employment for those aged 20–24 of 32% to 20%; and for those aged 25–29, of 59% to 40%. For these newer and younger teachers, 'relationships are not only difficult to develop over the disjointed and relatively short-term engagements common for early career replacement teachers, but they are undermined by the common lack of authority and experience of early career teachers' (Preston 2019, 181). Indeed, 'casual beginning teachers' have been noted in the literature to commonly go without the kind of support, induction and professional development provided for permanent staff members and are rarely accorded the same respect (Bamberry 2011; McCormack and Thomas 2005; Mercieca 2017; Nicholas and Wells 2017). The impacts of casual and fixed-term employment for young teachers are also felt beyond the school environment, with difficulty securing things like bank loans and finding appropriate accommodation, if there is uncertainty around employment security in a particular location (Mercieca 2017). Drawing on a sample exclusively of early career teachers, Jenkins, Smith, and Maxwell (2009, 76) warn that 'potentially very effective teachers will be lost to the profession', demoralised by the uncertain prospect of permanency.

### Understanding precariousness in fixed-term employment

Preston's (2019) work on precariousness in teaching, cited above, draws on labour market segmentation research that differentiates between primary labour markets (with high income and job security) and secondary labour markets (with low income and job security). Preston argues that fixed-term 'replacement teaching' usually falls into the category of secondary labour markets, making it 'an unattractive "bad job"' (Preston 2019, 177). Yet Preston notes distinctions here, too. If one is repeatedly hired at the same school you are part of an *internal, organisation-led* secondary labour market which allows the development of social capital and professional networks, and recognition of skills. Those who are hired in casual or fixed-term positions across multiple schools operate within an *external, market-led* secondary labour market, which limits their capacity for networking, relationship-building and professional recognition.

Such nuances are clearly important in understanding experiences of precarious work and can be considered part of what is broadly referred to in employment relations literature as 'job quality'. Burgess and Connell (2019) suggest that the numerous elements of job quality can be captured under four broad dimensions: *job prospects* (e.g. including job security and career progression); *extrinsic job quality* (e.g. pay and benefits and occupational health and safety); *intrinsic job quality* (e.g. work organisation, skill development/recognition and supervision and organisational support); and *working time quality* (e.g. work scheduling discretion and the impacts on home/family life). This fourth dimension underlines that the impact of job quality extends beyond the health and well-being of the individual employee (Findlay, Kalleberg, and Warhurst 2013, 447) and acknowledges impact on 'the health and well-being of employees' children, relationships and household life' (Knox, Warhurst, and Pocock 2011, 8).

Given the wide range of factors that can be taken into account, it is therefore important to note that job quality has also been described as 'very much a contextual phenomenon', and largely dependent 'on the amount of choice a person has over the kinds of jobs s/he can obtain' (Findlay, Kalleberg, and Warhurst 2013, 448). Indeed, according to Loughlin and Murray (2013, 532), 'job status congruence' is important – that is, whether employees are 'working full-time, contract, or part-time *by choice*' (emphasis in original). Thus Preston (2019) notes that for some, casual or fixed-term work can be a 'good job' where it is part of the primary labour market, with those in such roles (e.g. consultants) having authority and status as recognised 'specialist' professionals.

The impact of precariousness has also been considered in relation to the concept of labour market 'scarring', a metaphor from labour market segmentation literature which sees bad jobs as having long term 'scarring effects', reducing skills and future earnings (e.g. Taubman and Wachter 1986; Burchell and Rubery 1990). Teachers working in temporary employment may experience less employer 'investment' in professional learning and development opportunities, which may 'scar' by impacting future employability (Mooi-Reci and Wooden 2017). However, as Egdell and Beck point out (2020, 7), most research on scarring has focused 'at the macro- and meso- levels'; it is also 'empirically useful to understand scarring from the perspective of those who experience unemployment and/or poor work'.

In this article, we contribute to addressing this gap through the exploration of both quantitative and qualitative data, considering not just 'what is precarious employment, but "what does precarious employment do"?' (Cuervo and Chesters 2019, 296). To our knowledge the question of what fixed-term contract precariousness 'does' to those in the field of education has yet to be explored. Given the newness of the temporary teaching category and the lack of attention it has thus far received in relation to such concepts as job quality and scarring, it is worth looking more closely at how work within this employment category is experienced by teachers. In the next section, we outline our approach to providing such an examination.

## Method

This article draws on data gathered via a large state-wide survey of teachers in NSW, Australia. The survey was not specific to teachers working in temporary positions, but rather aimed to gather the views of a representative sample of all public school teachers regarding the nature and experience of work and workload, as well as strategies to address such work. The large data set provides an opportunity to explore the category of temporary teaching – how it might compare to that of permanent staff in relation to workload, as well as how this relatively new category of employment may be experienced and understood by those within it. In a companion article, we draw in part on this survey to explore the category of temporary teaching as a manifestation of union strategy resulting in a process of decommodification and recommodification (McGrath-Champ et al. under review). Here, we provide deeper analyses of survey data, highlighting the impact on

EDUCATIONAL LEADERSHIP AND POLICY IN A TIME OF PRECARITY 59

and experiences of respondents in relation to 'scarring' and job quality, including apparent tensions between and within teaching staff and school leadership.

The survey on which we draw was commissioned and facilitated by the NSW Teachers' Federation (NSWTF) in 2018 (McGrath-Champ et al. 2018). A total of 34% of the union's membership completed the survey ($n = 18,234$). With the union representing 82% of all public school teachers in the state of NSW, this sample can be considered quite comprehensive. Of the sample, the proportion of teachers in temporary teaching roles (21%, $n = 3749$) very closely reflected their membership of the union (19%). Those in permanent positions (77%, $n = 13,969$) were slightly over-represented relative to union membership (63%) whilst those undertaking casual work (3%, $n = 506$) were under-represented (10%). The union membership figures across these three employment categories match recent government workforce profile data (CESE 2018).

In this article, we draw on quantitative data primarily in relation to demographic information as well as work hours and demands. In addition, we explore qualitative responses to the three main open-ended items in the survey, analysed via a combination of content analysis and thematic analysis (Ezzy 2003). Content analysis based on the shorthand term 'temp*' captured abbreviated and full use of the word 'temporary', raised by those who were themselves currently in temporary employment. Mentions of 'temp*' that were not referring to the temporary teacher employment category were excluded. Questions and numbers of responses from teachers employed in a temporary capacity and mentioning 'temp*' in relation to such employment are as follows:

- 'Please feel free to comment on any changes to your workload over the last 5 years (2013–2018)': $n = 55$
- 'Please feel free to provide any other ideas you think would support you in your work': $n = 51$
- 'Please provide any additional comments you would like to make in relation to your work in schools or other workplaces. We are keen to hear your perspective': $n = 112$

We note that these questions did not ask about temporary work specifically, meaning that those who referred to temporary teaching voluntarily raised this issue. The resulting qualitative data were coded thematically, as presented below.

## Results and discussion

### *Workload in temporary teaching*

In our sample, teachers in temporary employment reported very similar demands in their work to permanent teachers. Teachers in temporary roles estimated working an average of 56 h per week during term time, compared to 57 for those in permanent positions and 40 for those employed as casuals. Figure 1 represents reported increases in: hours; complexity of work; administrative tasks; and collection, analysis and reporting of data across permanent, temporary and casual staff.

It is evident that high percentages of respondents report work increases across all employment types. However, they are markedly higher for employees in permanent and temporary positions than for those in casual positions. This finding highlights the

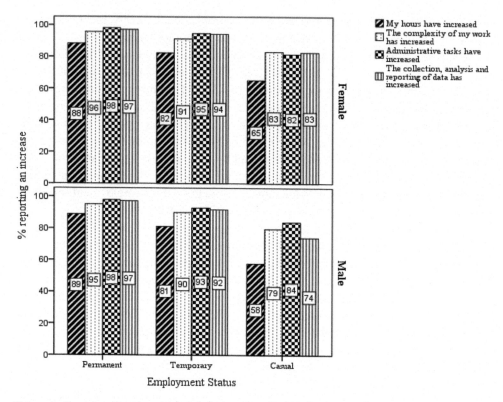

**Figure 1.** Changes to work and employment status – past 5 years.

importance of examining the category of temporary teaching as distinct from casual work.

That there are, however, marginally lower proportions of respondents in temporary roles reporting increases in these dimensions of workload compared to permanent staff may reflect the fact that the temporary staff members are a younger average age (37 years, compared to 45 years for permanent and 48 years for casual, reflecting patterns also reported in McKenzie et al. 2014). This may make it difficult to perceive change over what may be a more limited period of time in the workforce. Indeed, comments in the qualitative data suggest this is at least partly the case; one respondent noted that it was 'difficult to comment [on change in workload over the past five years] as I have been in various casual and temporary roles over that time', or that they are 'a new teacher so I can't really comment on changes'.

In addition, the pattern of those in temporary employment reporting similar, but slightly lower levels and impact of workload is also borne out in reported 'work demands', as depicted in Table 1. Here we see very similar – and high – reports from both permanent and temporary respondents. However, these figures are rather different from those in casual employment, which sit consistently lower, perhaps indicating teachers in temporary positions experience poorer *working time quality* and *intrinsic job quality* than teachers working casually. In contrast, it is evident that there are lower percentages of permanent and temporary staff reporting often or always having enough time to complete their work tasks. The lower work demands reported by those in casual

## EDUCATIONAL LEADERSHIP AND POLICY IN A TIME OF PRECARITY 61

**Table 1.** Employment status and work demands.

| | | Employment Status | | |
| --- | --- | --- | --- | --- |
| | | Permanent % | Temporary % | Casual % |
| Does your work require you to work or think very quickly? | Never | 0 | 0 | 0 |
| | Rarely | 0 | 0 | 1 |
| | Sometimes | 4 | 4 | 5 |
| | Often | 30 | 28 | 33 |
| | Always | 66 | 68 | 61 |
| Does your work require you to work very hard? | Never | 0 | 0 | 0 |
| | Rarely | 0 | 0 | 1 |
| | Sometimes | 3 | 3 | 7 |
| | Often | 26 | 26 | 34 |
| | Always | 72 | 70 | 58 |
| Does your work require too great an effort on your part? | Never | 0 | 0 | 1 |
| | Rarely | 2 | 3 | 6 |
| | Sometimes | 25 | 25 | 39 |
| | Often | 36 | 35 | 28 |
| | Always | 36 | 37 | 27 |
| Do you have enough time to complete your work tasks? | Never | 24 | 20 | 9 |
| | Rarely | 42 | 42 | 31 |
| | Sometimes | 28 | 31 | 37 |
| | Often | 4 | 6 | 18 |
| | Always | 1 | 1 | 5 |
| Does your work impose contradictory requirements on you? | Never | 3 | 4 | 7 |
| | Rarely | 8 | 12 | 10 |
| | Sometimes | 44 | 46 | 47 |
| | Often | 33 | 28 | 25 |
| | Always | 12 | 10 | 10 |

employment suggest that in some ways, at least in terms of workload, it can be a less intensive role.

While work hours and demands are generally similar between teachers in permanent and temporary employment, there are also some small but important differences in particular work tasks undertaken. For instance, teachers in temporary employment are more likely to plan lessons (90%), differentiate curriculum (87%) and complete marking (65%) as part of their daily labour than those in permanent employment (82%, 79% and 54% respectively). These teachers were also more likely to be running extra-curricular activities as a daily activity (21% temporary, 18% permanent). On the other hand, some daily activities are more likely to be done by those in permanent roles, such as liaising with external agencies (14% permanent vs 8% temporary).

Considering these data as a whole, it is evident that teachers in temporary employment in NSW public schools are doing similar amounts of work to those in permanent employment, but with some differences in the nature of that work. Qualitative data indicate that teachers in temporary employment feel as though they are doing as much, if not more than their permanent counterparts. This was the second most dominant theme in responses to the open-ended question regarding changes to workload over time, raised by twelve out of 55 respondents. As one succinctly put it, 'I work as hard if not harder than many permanent teachers'. Indeed, for some there seemed to be a perception that those in temporary roles needed to do more, particularly in relation to extra-curricular activities – which supports the quantitative finding on this noted above. As one respondent commented: 'there is a huge expectation that teachers put their hand up for extra roles … which adds to the pressure teachers (particularly temp teachers as we do more) feel'.

This issue of those in temporary positions feeling as though they work as hard, or harder than those in permanent roles was also raised by ten out of 112 respondents in the final open-ended question of the survey. Here, one expressed frustration about 'temporary teachers who are valuable but not deemed worthy of permanent employment' and yet 'who work just the same as the permanent teachers'. Another commented:

> I don't understand why I am treated differently to permanent staff when my workload is exactly the same. Very unfair. The only difference is that my stress levels are HIGHER because there is no certainty … and I know that the department does not value me or care about me at all. All I am is a number.

There is clear frustration and a perception of injustice in these comments, as temporary employment '[closes] the door on the ability to plan for the future' (Cuervo and Chesters 2019, 307), with the uncertain prospect of permanency and a sense of being undervalued having a demoralising effect (Jenkins, Smith, and Maxwell 2009). This indicates how poor job quality, characterised by poor *job prospects* and *intrinsic job quality*, for teachers employed on a temporary basis can have unique 'scarring' effects for the future. Only two comments across the three sets of open-ended responses indicated anything positive about being in a temporary position. One of these was from a respondent that had recently moved from casual to temporary, which had meant some improvement in security and regularity of work; another was from a former Assistant Principal, who had moved to being a temporary classroom teacher to reduce workload (confounding employment category with role). In the following section, we explore these frustrations of employees in temporary work further, and discuss how this sense of needing to do as much or more than permanent staff members may be due to a particular need to 'prove' oneself to school leadership.

### *Temporary teaching and school leadership*

Indeed, one reason why those in temporary employment may feel they have to do 'more' than those in permanent positions related to having to 'prove yourself'. This was the most dominant theme in responses to the question about changes to workload over the past five years, raised by 24 out of the 55 respondents who commented on their temporary status. As one respondent put it, 'temporary teachers … feel they need to 'prove themselves' better teachers in order to gain permanent employment'. Another expressed:

> I feel there is an unspoken pressure for temp teachers to 'do more' in order to heighten their chances to get work for the next year. This results in temp teachers to take on extra workload and may result in being overworked and stressed.

Permanent teachers, on the other hand, were perceived to be able to afford to do less, with one respondent reporting that 'two permanent teachers have even stated, "I don't have to do anything else I am already permanent"'. There is a perverse relationship with school leadership indicated here. The need to 'do more' and 'prove yourself' is to impress the school principal and hopefully have your contract renewed or even converted into a permanent position. This may reflect a desire to avoid relegation to the external secondary labour market which might see them bounced across different schools rather than maintaining work within just one (Preston 2019). Respondents expressing this theme felt they had 'become the silenced workers that say YES to everything that is put to us', feeling that they 'cannot say no' as 'principals have ultimate power'. As the quote in the title of this article indicates, teachers' careers were felt to be 'at the whim of principals who pick and choose according to who toes the line … jumping through hoops to retain their position and add to their CV in order to gain permanency'. This suggests impacts on job quality, particularly in relation to teachers' sense of control over their work, as they describe having to 'take whatever is handed to you' as 'workload rules go out the window'. Similar findings have been noted for 'substitute' teachers in Canada (The Alberta Teachers' Association 2011), for teachers on fixed-term contracts in Victoria (Feather and Rauter 2004) and for teachers working in casual positions in NSW (Charteris, Jenkins, Jones, et al. 2017). It would seem the need to continually 'prove' oneself means that teachers in temporary positions experience poor *intrinsic job quality*, compounded by poor *job prospects*.

It is possible that experiences of precariousness can also impact teachers' relationships with other school staff as also noted in Preston (2019), highlighting the importance of recognising what precarious employment 'does' to those who experience it (Cuervo and Chesters 2019). This includes relationships with other teachers in temporary positions; one respondent perceived that 'temp staff are constantly working against each other in an uneasy one-upmanship to try and secure a full time position'. Another respondent explained that they felt 'being a temporary teacher is something that is consistently held over my head', causing them to 'have to increase my workload to ensure that I am a more desirable employee, and someone they would keep over others'. This also suggests an experience of exploitation, as permanent staff members and/or executive 'prey' on temporary teachers by '[shifting] work' to them, echoing research about the 'othering' of those in casual employment within schools (Charteris, Jenkins, Bannister-Tyrrell, et al. 2017).

Furthermore, our quantitative data suggest that a large proportion of temporary teachers are in their first decade of teaching and relatively young, working on average for more than four years in one school, and engaging in distinct efforts to maintain their contracts and/or convert to permanency. In Table 2 we see that temporary teachers have lower averages for the number of years working in their current school and their total years as a teacher. There is a statistically significant association between employment categories and the number of years working at current schools (ANOVA, $F = 10.22$, $p = .01$). Approximately 50% of temporary teachers have been working at their current school for four years or more. National data suggest that the proportion of temporary employment

**Table 2.** Employment status and years of teaching experience.

| | | Employment Status | | | |
|---|---|---|---|---|---|
| | | Permanent | Temporary | Casual | Total |
| Years working as a teacher, consultant or other position at this school/workplace | Mean | 12 | 6 | 11 | 12 |
| | Median | 10 | 4 | 5 | 10 |
| | Range | 57 | 48 | 50 | 57 |
| Years working as a teacher, consultant or other position related to education in total | Mean | 17 | 9 | 17 | 17 |
| | Median | 16 | 6 | 11 | 16 |
| | Range | 57 | 50 | 52 | 57 |

among young teachers (< 30 years) is 35%, much higher than the average of 14% (Thomson and Hillman 2020).

There may also be a gendered dynamic to understanding these experiences of temporary teaching and its relation to school leadership. OECD data, based on lower-secondary schools, indicates that the percentage of women who are principals in such schools in Australia (40%) is not proportional to those employed as teachers (62%) (OECD 2019). Overall, in our data, more teachers identifying as male (81%) reported being in permanent employment than did those identifying as female (75.5%), with fewer men reporting temporary employment (male 16%; female 21.9%). There is a statistically significant relationship between gender and employment category (chi-Squared = 61.154, $p < .05$) with women much more likely to be temporary and men more likely to be permanent. This results in nearly as many women in our sample employed as temporary teachers ($n$ = 3066, 17% of total teachers) as men in permanent employment ($n$ = 3162).

Figure 2 shows the age distribution of employment category by gender and suggests that women may also stay longer as temporary teachers than men do. Substantial proportions of temporary women teachers are seen in the 40–60 years age bracket, while among men the peak numbers of temporary employment, seen around 30 years of age (as with women), shows a more rapid drop off in older age groups. Further research is needed to confirm whether this reflects men moving up and out of temporary positions, and potentially on to leadership positions more quickly. Indeed, recent research has indicated that proportionally more men receive promotions in the NSW public school teacher workforce (McGrath 2020), suggesting gendered implications for *job prospects*.

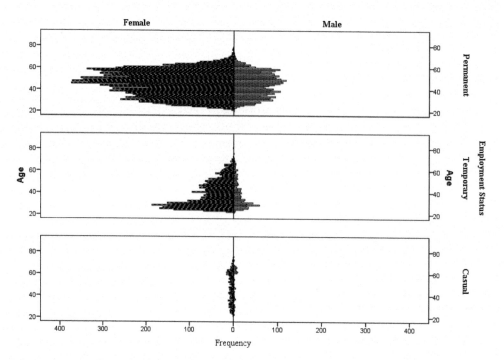

**Figure 2.** Employment status, gender and age.

Possibly, the different gender likelihood and age structure of permanency may be due to perceptions of teaching as a 'feminised' profession and a bias, unconscious or otherwise, towards hiring men in permanent roles. Mooi-Reci and Wooden (2017, 1086) suggest that Australia-wide, women are 'expected to have fragmented employment careers', and thus experience less long-term wage scarring as a consequence of casual employment. However, our data indicate that in the case of the 'feminised' profession of teaching, there may indeed be a scarring effect of temporary employment for women, with an impact not only on wages via promotion opportunities, but also the job content and professional development opportunities attendant to such positions. Given the relative imbalance in school leadership, the 'conversion' of proportionally and absolutely more women teachers to permanent status may be one way in which to help redress this dynamic.

A final related theme within the qualitative data was dissatisfaction with the current process for gaining permanency. There was a perception that the 'merit selection' process, with one in two permanent positions now selected locally (Gavin and McGrath-Champ 2017), was 'unethical' and 'very unfair', with 'employment of temporary teachers on perception rather than merit'. This dissatisfaction was raised in open-response questions about change over time (6/55) and strategies (3/51), as well as the final open comment question (15/112). A small number ($n = 3$) of temporary teacher participants explicitly linked this dissatisfaction with employment processes to the recent LSLD policy reform. One stated that 'Since Local Schools Local Decisions, "power has gone to the heads" of principals and some executives'. Some respondents also expressed frustration with the practice of hiring 'targeted graduates' straight out of university into permanent positions, seeing this policy as 'very unfair as new graduates are given priority to those who have been working for 10 years or more'. Respondents suggested that the Department of Education provide 'more opportunities for temp staff to become permanent'. This recommendation, to convert temporary status positions to permanent, was the most prominent theme in open-ended responses to the question about strategies for workload management, raised by 30 out of the 51 who commented on the temporary category, and 30 out of 112 who mentioned temporary teaching when responding to the final open-ended question. In addition, quantitative data suggest that only 27% of those in temporary employment were working in that capacity by choice, indicating a lack of 'job status congruence', with teachers in temporary employment feeling 'trapped' within their work arrangements (Loughlin and Murray 2013, 532) and experiencing compounding pressures of poor *intrinsic job quality* and *job prospects* brought on by a mode of governance that elevates leader discretion and which has longer term 'scarring' effects.

## Implications and conclusion

Temporary teaching, a relatively new employment category in NSW public schools, is on the rise and has not yet received much academic attention. Yet it would seem that such attention is warranted, especially given that previous documentation on precarious work in teaching often considers fixed-term contract work either as a version of casual work (e.g. Bamberry 2011), or alternatively, considers it to be 'like' permanent employment by virtue of including leave entitlements (ABS 2019). Contrary to these categorisations, our data indicate that temporary teaching work is not like casual work – the hours and demands are considerably higher, and very similar to those reported by permanent staff. Yet temporary teaching is also experienced differently to permanent teachers' work, with the development of interpersonal fault-lines between temporary and permanent members of staff, and between teachers and school leadership. Overall, our findings indicate that teachers in temporary positions experience most of the dimensions of job quality (Burgess and Connell 2019) negatively; working harder than they wish to and feeling insecure in their roles, while also facing poorer job prospects and the potential for future employment 'scarring'. Our analysis further revealed a gendered dimension. Women are more likely to be temporary employees, and there are indications that women may be in temporary employment for longer than men, thereby bearing the impact of scarring more extensively.

To resolve these issues, principals might consider their work with employees in temporary roles and ensure that they, or other permanent staff in the school, do not take advantage of this vulnerability through delegation of work, the 'dangling' of employment contracts or the local appointment of staff based on reasons other than merit. However, with schools being highly pressured environments for all staff (McGrath-Champ et al. 2018), including principals, such recommendations are unlikely to have lasting or widespread impact. Instead, change must come from above, with the upward trend in proportion of fixed-term contract positions actively reversed and priority given to those who have worked in a temporary capacity for greater periods of time, with a proportional gender balance. As Preston (2019, 178) notes, 'even though replacement work is required for many reasons, it does not have to be undertaken by teachers in insecure employment'. These recommendations are only a beginning, but finding ways for policy-makers to address the issues raised in this article is important in optimising professional capacity, protecting the leadership pipeline and the future of work in schools. Teachers new to the profession must be supported, to enable effective leadership in the future as well as positive interpersonal dynamics within our schools in the present.

## Disclosure statement

No potential conflict of interest was reported by the author(s).

## Funding

This work was supported by NSW Teachers Federation.

## ORCID

*Meghan Stacey* ⓘ http://orcid.org/0000-0003-2192-9030
*Scott Fitzgerald* ⓘ http://orcid.org/0000-0001-9043-9727
*Rachel Wilson* ⓘ http://orcid.org/0000-0002-2550-1253
*Susan McGrath-Champ* ⓘ http://orcid.org/0000-0002-2209-5683
*Mihajla Gavin* ⓘ http://orcid.org/0000-0001-6796-5198

## References

ABS (Australian Bureau of Statistics). 2019. *6333.0 Characteristics of Employment, Australia*. https://www.abs.gov.au/ausstats/abs@.nsf/mf/6333.0.
The Alberta Teachers' Association. 2011. *Substitute Teachers in Alberta: A Research Report*. Edmonton, Canada: The Alberta Teachers' Association.
Bamberry, L. 2011. "'As Disposable as the Next Tissue out of the Box ... ': Casual Teaching and job Quality in New South Wales Public School Education." *Journal of Industrial Relations* 53 (1): 49–64.
Burchell, B., and J. Rubery. 1990. "An Empirical Investigation into the Segmentation of the Labour Supply." *Work, Employment and Society* 4 (4): 551–575.
Burgess, J., and J. Connell. 2019. "Using Case Study Research to Capture the Quality of Working Lives." In *Handbook of Research Methods on the Quality of Working Lives*, edited by D. Wheatley, 141–162. Cheltenham: Edward Elgar.
CESE (Centre for Education Statistics and Evaluation). 2018. "Workforce profile of the NSW teaching profession 2016." https://www.cese.nsw.gov.au/publications-filter/workforce-profile-of-the-nsw-teaching-profession-2016.
Charteris, J., K. Jenkins, M. Bannister-Tyrrell, and M. Jones. 2017. "Structural Marginalisation, Othering and Casual Relief Teacher Subjectivities." *Critical Studies in Education* 58 (1): 104–119.
Charteris, J., K. Jenkins, M. Jones, and M. Bannister-Tyrrell. 2017. "Discourse Appropriation and Category Boundary Work: Casual Teachers in the Market." *Discourse: Studies in the Cultural Politics of Education* 38 (4): 511–529. doi:10.1080/01596306.2015.1113158.
Cuervo, H., and J. Chesters. 2019. "The [im]Possibility of Planning a Future: How Prolonged Precarious Employment During Transitions Affects the Lives of Young Australians." *Labour and Industry: A Journal of the Social and Economic Relations of Work* 29 (4): 295–312.
Cuervo, H., and J. Wyn. 2016. "An Unspoken Crisis: The 'Scarring Effects' of the Complex Nexus Between Education and Work on Two Generations of Young Australians." *International Journal of Lifelong Education* 35 (2): 122–135. doi:10.1080/02601370.2016.1164467.
Egdell, V., and V. Beck. 2020. "A Capability Approach to Understand the Scarring Effects of Unemployment and Job Insecurity: Developing the Research Agenda." *Work, Employment and Society*. doi:10.1177/0950017020909042.
Ezzy, D. 2003. *Qualitative Analysis*. Hoboken: Taylor and Francis.
Feather, N. T., and K. A. Rauter. 2004. "Organizational Citizenship Behaviours in Relation to job Status, Job Insecurity, Organizational Commitment and Identification, Job Satisfaction and Work Values." *Journal of Occupational and Organizational Psychology* 77: 81–94.

Findlay, P., A. L. Kalleberg, and C. Warhurst. 2013. "The Challenge of job Quality." *Human Relations* 66 (4): 441–451. doi:10.1177/0018726713481070.

Gavin, M., and S. McGrath-Champ. 2017. "Devolving Authority: The Impact of Giving Public Schools Power to Hire Staff." *Asia Pacific Journal of Human Resources* 55: 255–274. doi:10.1111/1744-7941.12110.

Jenkins, K., H. Smith, and T. Maxwell. 2009. "Challenging Experiences Faced by Beginning Casual Teachers: Here One Day and Gone the Next!." *Asia Pacific Journal of Education* 37 (1): 63–78.

Knox, A., C. Warhurst, and B. Pocock. 2011. "Job Quality Matters." *Journal of Industrial Relations* 53 (1): 5–11. doi:10.1177/0022185610390293.

Lierich, D., and C. O'Connor. 2009. "The Effect of Fixed-Term Contracts on Rural Secondary Teachers." *International Employment Relations Review* 15 (2): 58–82.

Loughlin, C., and R. Murray. 2013. "Employment Status Congruence and Job Quality." *Human Relations* 66 (4): 529–553. doi:10.1177/0018726712460705.

McCormack, A., and K. Thomas. 2005. "The Reality of Uncertainty: The Plight of Casual Beginning Teachers." *Change: Transformations in Education* 8 (1): 17–31.

McGrath-Champ, S., S. Fitzgerald, M. Gavin, M. Stacey, and R. Wilson. Under Review. "Commodification Processes in the Employment Heartland: Temporary Teachers' Experiences of Work and Workload." *Work, Employment and Society*.

McGrath-Champ, S., R. Wilson, M. Stacey, and S. Fitzgerald. 2018. *Understanding Work in Schools*. https://www.nswtf.org.au/files/18438_uwis_digital.pdf.

McGrath, K. 2020. "When Female Leaders Outnumber Men: The Decline of Male School Principals in Australia." *Journal of Gender Studies* 29 (5): 604–612.

McKenzie, P., P. Weldon, G. Rowley, M. Murphy, and J. McMillan. 2014. *Staff in Australia's Schools 2013: Main Report on the Survey*. Melbourne, Australia: ACER.

Mercieca, B. 2017. "What are we Doing to our Early Career Teachers? The Issue of the Casualisation of the Teaching Workforce." *Australian Educational Leader* 39 (1): 38–41.

Mooi-Reci, I., and M. Wooden. 2017. "Casual Employment and Long-Term Wage Outcomes." *Human Relations* 70 (9): 1064–1090. doi:10.1177/0018726716686666.

Nicholas, M., and M. Wells. 2017. "Insights Into Casual Relief Teaching: Casual Relief Teachers' Perceptions of Their Knowledge and Skills." *Asia-Pacific Journal of Teacher Education* 45 (3): 229–249. doi:10.1080/1359866X.2016.1169506.

NSW Department of Education. 2020. *Casual and Temporary Teaching*. https://education.nsw.gov.au/about-us/careers-at-education/roles-and-locations/roles-at-education/teaching/casual-and-temporary-teaching.

NSW Government. 2020. *Staffing Agreement 2020-21*. https://education.nsw.gov.au/about-us/careers-at-education/roles-and-locations/roles-at-education/teaching/staffing-agreement.

OECD. 2014. *The OECD Teaching and Learning International Survey (TALIS) 2013: results - excel figures and tables*. http://www.oecd.org/education/school/talis-excel-figures-and-tables.htm.

OECD. 2019. *Country note - Australia*. http://www.oecd.org/education/talis/TALIS2018_CN_AUS.pdf.

O'Sullivan, M., J. Lavelle, T. Turner, J. McMahon, C. Murphy, L. Ryan, and P. Gunnigle. 2020. "Employer-Led Flexibility, Working Time Uncertainty, and Trade Union Responses: The Case of Academics, Teachers and School Secretaries in Ireland." *Journal of Industrial Relations*, doi:10.1177/0022185620960198.

Preston, B. 2019. "Reforming Replacement Teaching: A Game Changer for the Development of Early Career Teaching?" In *Attracting and Keeping the Best Teachers*, edited by A. Sullivan, B. Johnson, and M. Simons, 161–190. Singapore: Springer Nature.

Taubman, P., and M. Wachter. 1986. "Segmented Labor Markets." In *Handbook of Labor Economics*, edited by O. C. Ashenfelter, and R. Layardm, 1183–1217. New York: North-Holland.

Thomson, S., and K. Hillman. 2020. *The Teaching and Learning International Survey 2018. Australian Report Volume 2: Teachers and School Leaders as Valued Professionals*. https://research.acer.edu.au/talis/7/.

# Embracing vulnerability: how has the Covid-19 pandemic affected the pressures school leaders in Northern England face and how they deal with them?

Michael Jopling and Oliver Harness

**ABSTRACT**
Research into the effects of pressure on school leaders has focused more on its impacts at the system level than on the human impact on leaders. Using theories of vulnerability, this paper attempts to redress this balance, examining the challenges school leaders in North East England faced during the initial phase of the Covid-19 pandemic and the support they accessed. Combining an online survey of 132 school leaders with in-depth interviews, the study found that the pandemic had an amplifying effect, increasing both leaders' responsibilities and the pressure on them. It also found that many find it difficult to admit when they are under pressure and have no source of support. This suggests new ways need to be found to help all leaders, and particularly male and secondary leaders, to embrace their vulnerability, access professional support, and increase schools' focus on the mental health of children and adults.

While pressures on schools and school leaders to maintain standards and improve attainment continue to increase (Simkins et al. 2018), research still largely focuses on their effects at the system level, examining issues such as improving succession planning and recruitment (Bush 2011; NAHT 2019), rather than the human impact on school leaders as individuals. Drawing on theories of vulnerability, this paper attempts to redress the balance, examining the effects on leaders of policy emphasis on school 'self-improvement' in England, whether the Covid-19 pandemic has increased, or reduced, pressures on leaders, and the extent to which it offers an opportunity to rethink schools. The research focused on exploring the perspectives of school leaders working in the North East of England in order to explore in depth the contextual factors which affect them. Its contribution is to use vulnerability theory to try to understand the challenges and responses of school leaders during a period of unprecedented crisis.

## Context: the English school system

While characteristics associated with neoliberalism such as high levels of accountability, marketisation and competition can be found in education systems across the world, schools and school leaders in England face a particularly intense set of pressures (Ball 2017). A strict school inspection regime and school league tables were introduced in the early 1990s, followed by many school improvement initiatives aimed to improve 'failing' schools with the result that many leaders still feel they are one inspection judgement away from dismissal (Thompson, Lingard, and Ball 2020). From 2010 schools were incentivised to become academies, publicly funded schools which are independent of local authority (LA) oversight and held accountable directly by the Department for Education. Government statistics show that 78% of secondary schools and 37% of primary schools had become academies by January 2021. Many are grouped into one of the 1170 multi-academy trusts (MATs) that currently manage two or more academies, overseen by a CEO and a single board of trustees. The *Importance of Teaching* (DfE 2010), the White Paper which introduced these changes, represented them as increasing autonomy and school to school support to create a 'self-improving' school system. Hargreaves' (2010) early conceptual work identified its four building blocks of collaborative school clusters; a local solutions approach; co-construction between schools; and system leaders operating across schools and localities.

Combined with the austerity measures and budget cuts which severely reduced local government funding and capacity from 2010, this is the policy context in which this research into the pressures school leaders face was conducted. The North East of England was selected for the research because some areas have high levels of poverty and disadvantage, which are associated with increasing pressures on schools, and because schools there have been held to underperform in comparison with other regions, although the evidence for that, especially at primary level, has been contested (Jopling 2018).

## Literature review: precarity, isolation and vulnerability among school leaders

For school leaders in England, the precarity of their position derives from the unrelenting pressure to improve standards and results already cited. It has long been a feature of school leadership research, in England and elsewhere, that excessive demands, pressure and burnouts have been associated with a real or impending crisis in recruitment and retention (Bush 2011). Almost 20 years ago, Ginsberg and Gray Davies (2003) found that little research had focused explicitly on the effects of emotional experiences on leaders. While this is no longer the case, Berkovich and Eyal's (2015) review of the international evidence about educational leaders and emotions between 1992 and 2012 identified only 49 studies for analysis. They highlighted three core themes: the factors influencing the leaders' emotions; leaders' behaviours and their effects on followers' emotions; and leaders' emotional abilities. The smaller evidence base relating to England has tended to focus on the third of these areas. For example, in a study of primary school leaders Crawford (2007, 96) identified the polarisation between the apparent rationality of leadership effectiveness and a growing focus on leaders' need for emotional intelligence, concluding that: 'Research into emotion in educational leadership can enable educational leaders to examine the way they handle their own emotions, how that interacts with the emotional climate of a school and the implications for their own leadership'. This echoed similar findings from Beatty (2000) and Zorn and Boler

(2007). Steward (2014) focused on how leaders in three English local authorities (LAs) developed emotional resilience, identifying the key roles played by leaders' early influences and the importance of both energy and agency in helping leaders cope with the challenges they face, This was countered by Morrison and Ecclestone (2011) who argued against excessive concentration on the emotional elements of leadership in leadership development programmes, particularly if that meant they did not 'question the structures and activities of current educational practices or are used to downgrade cognitive and substantive knowledge and skills'.

Connected with this is the longstanding literature relating to headteacher isolation (Jones 1994; Dussault and Thibodeau 1997). Recent research has focused on exploring the multidimensional nature of isolation and a similarly complex set of ameliorating factors. For example, Howard and Mallory (2008) identified the need for effective personal and professional support systems and social support from colleagues, alongside factors such as having a strong sense of purpose, distributing leadership, and ensuring they have time for family and friends. Similarly, in their study of headteacher burnout, Stephenson and Bauer (2010) emphasised the complexity of isolation as a variable and found that while research has associated reduced teacher isolation with improved student outcomes, less attention has been paid to its impact on school leaders. They also found that reducing burnout should involve both reducing role overload and ensuring social support, but that facilitating supplementary collaboration (central to the kinds of school-to-school support promoted in England) among leaders working at distance from each other is difficult. Reflecting this and other previous research (e.g. Izgar 2009), Tahir et al.'s (2017) examination of new headteachers in Malaysia found that isolation was a feature of the early stages of becoming a leader and focused on its causes and strategies to overcome it, rather than its effects. They found that female leaders and those working in urban primary schools felt more isolated, but that isolation was relatively short-lived and could be overcome by mentoring (a common finding, contradicted by Stephenson and Bauer (2010) albeit in relation to coaching); constant interaction with other teachers; and including socialisation strategies in training. However, they also found that other leaders' unwillingness to share knowledge and ideas contributed to their sense of isolation. Berkovich and Eyal's (2015, 140) review found that some leaders' attempts to reduce their isolation by discussing their emotions with staff 'increased their sense of vulnerability'. This is an issue that requires further investigation.

### *Approaching and embracing vulnerability*

Salvatore and McVarish (2014) begin their metalogue on vulnerability with the recognition of the negativity of dictionary definitions of vulnerability, which focus on openness to attack or criticism. This should be seen against the backdrop of what has been identified as a 'vulnerability zeitgeist' in social policy in recent years (Ecclestone and Rawdin 2016), as groups, families or young people characterised as 'vulnerable' have become subject to a range of intervention programmes in the UK, Europe and North America. This has been reflected in education in the ways in which students previously described as 'disadvantaged', 'under-achieving' or having special educational needs or a disability have been recategorized as 'vulnerable' and schools monitor their progress carefully. In the English context this was evident in the 13 uses of the word in *The*

*Importance of Teaching* (DfE 2010), which introduced the notion of the self-improving school system. It is difficult not to conclude with Potter and Brotherton (2013) that this ubiquity has effectively neutralised 'vulnerability' in policy. It has also exacerbated its negative connotations and increased the pressure on schools and school leaders to improve provision for and the achievement of students so classified.

The utility and appropriateness of applying the term 'vulnerable' in this way have been criticised for reflecting the growing therapeutic emphasis in social justice and education and diverting resources away from those most in need by Ecclestone and Hayes (2019). However, they also counsel against 'the construction of the idea of human beings as vulnerable and diminished that is being strengthened through therapeutic education' (Ecclestone and Hayes (2019, 22). This negative conceptualisation of vulnerability is also common in the body of research that has developed exploring vulnerability in teachers and, less commonly, in school leaders. Kelchtermans (1996, 312) influential work identifies vulnerability as a structural issue 'when teachers feel powerless or politically ineffective in the micro-political struggles about their desired workplace conditions', rather than as a primarily emotional or experiential condition. He suggests that teachers' experience vulnerability at various levels: in the classroom; in school in response to the demands and expectations of colleagues, leaders and parents; and beyond that in response to policy changes. Applying this to school leaders, Kelchtermans, Piot, and Ballet (2011) portray them as gatekeepers, also beset by similarly varying demands, whose vulnerability is related to their position caught between 'loneliness and belonging'. These conceptualisations are important but remain restricted in their view of vulnerability. This elision of the notion of vulnerability with being diminished or 'at risk', which much practice in schools in relation to vulnerable young people seems (often unintentionally) to perpetuate, obscures the potential for vulnerability to be regarded more positively. Doing so may help school leaders both to reject the deficit thinking associated with the term and to cope with the challenges they face.

Kelchtermans (2005) ends another study by suggesting that vulnerability should both endured and 'embraced', which points towards Angel's (2021, 132) warning in a rather different context that resisting vulnerability risks closing off the self:

> When you feel vulnerable, it's tempting to brace yourself against vulnerability – the fantasy of hardening yourself so that nothing can hurt you. The collateral, however, is that nothing can reach you, either.

This echoes Bullough's (2005, 23) study of teachability and vulnerability in which he directly addresses the negative connotations of the latter term in asserting that 'To be vulnerable is to be capable of being hurt, but to be invulnerable, if such a state is possible, is to limit the potential for learning'. He suggests that a balance needs to be struck to ensure that the 'burden of vulnerability' does not become too great for teachers and to allow them, and their students, to take risks. In a recent revision of the earlier paper, he added that is most likely to occur 'within a committed professional community and least likely in isolation' (Bullough 2019, 117). This has important implications for school leaders, given the tension between isolation and belonging identified by Kelchtermans, Piot, and Ballet (2011). Referencing Bullough (2005), Salvatore and McVarish (2014, 49) reject negative definitions of vulnerability and suggest that 'vulnerability in the classroom helps to establish a constructivist mindset, one that allows all participants in the room to learn.' This moves us towards a more active, even activist notion of vulnerability, which is captured in some extent in Ruck Simmonds' (2009) notion of 'critical vulnerability'. Drawing on Freire, Ruck Simmonds (2009, 84) describes this as as an act of resistance: 'To be critically vulnerable, therefore, implies a conscious recognition and willingness to transform society, and its institutions, into places where equity is experienced rather than considered'. She suggests that critical vulnerability requires an open approach focusing on cultivating strategic risk-taking, soulwork (reflective self-interrogation), creativity, and community-building.

These more positive (and critical) notions of vulnerability guided the analysis reported in this paper. The research explores whether encouraging school leaders to recognise the inherent vulnerability of their position as leaders and individuals might help them to deal with the stress and isolation which they often face. This is supported by the idea that the capacity to reflect in teaching, and leading teaching, is closely related to the acceptance of uncertainty. Dale and Frye (2009, 124) capture this in their hope that teachers remain learners in order to 'experience the joys and the delights as well as the discomforts and tensions of vulnerability and uncertainty'.

This suggests that relinquishing some control and acknowledging, even embracing their vulnerability may help leaders cope with the precarity and uncertainty of their position, resist enduring 'inspirational' leadership models (Ruck Simmonds 2009), and build stronger relationships with vulnerable young people in their schools. In order to do this, we need first to gain a much better understanding of the pressures school leaders feel they are under and how they deal with them. The research reported on here was designed to do this. Although it was conceived earlier, the fact that it was conducted during the early phases of the Covid-19 lockdown, which has intensified and magnified so many of the challenges which school leaders face, gave us a unique opportunity to explore leaders' experiences of extreme stress, vulnerability and new kinds of isolation and uncertainty with leaders in real-time.

## Methodology

The research questions behind this project, conceived before the pandemic struck, were:

- What challenges do school leaders face in North East England?
- Whom do they go to for support?

Following the pandemic, we refined the third research question, which initially focused on the factors associated with these challenges, to the following:

- How can we use this knowledge to rethink aspects of how schools work?

To address these questions, the research adopted a mixed methods design, combining a survey of school leaders (including deputy and assistant headteachers) in the North East of England with semi-structured interviews with five headteachers in three LAs in the region. The theoretical framework for the research applied theoretical constructions of vulnerability, such as those already discussed, to school leaders and was also informed by research into the self-improving school system (Greany and Higham 2018; Hadfield and Ainscow 2018).

The questionnaire survey was designed to collect leaders' immediate responses to the challenges of the COVID-19 lockdown quickly, the notion of collecting leaders' views in relation to areas such as perceived stress and the role of school leadership and collaboration quickly in real time took the school barometer surveys undertaken in Germany, Austria and Switzerland (Huber and Helm 2020) as an inspiration. It was piloted in May 2020 with a small group of school leaders not subsequently involved in the study, after which questions about autonomy and drop-down response menus were added, based on the responses and feedback. Informed by the literature reviewed, the survey explored the challenges leaders faced, the extent to which this put them under pressure and the support they draw on to cope. It also addressed issues of autonomy (and questions of trust and job satisfaction not reported in this paper), as well as whether and how they thought the pandemic represented an opportunity to rethink schools. It was distributed online in June and July 2020 to all schools in the North East of England with which we and our colleagues work as researchers, initial teacher educators and LA advisers in order to maximise the response rate before the summer break. Thus, the survey collected responses at the end of a school year in which the pandemic caused many schools to close after March except for children from key worker and 'vulnerable' families.

The interviews were conducted online late in 2020 to explore the issues identified in the survey in more depth and assess to what extent the autumn term of 2020/21 (when schools also closed) affected the experiences of the leaders interviewed. They were recruited through professional networks among headteachers and school improvement advisers in the region. Four of the leaders were primary headteachers and the fifth led a middle school. Five secondary headteachers in two LAs were also approached but were either too busy to participate or did not respond, which is understandable given the effects of the pandemic at the time. Our intention was always to draw on a relatively small sample in order to add depth to the survey outcomes while also minimising disruption to school leaders' work at a time of uncertainty and exhaustion.

### Sample

There are 858 schools in North East England. The questionnaire surveys were completed by 132 school leaders in 7 of the 12 LAs located in the region. Almost three-quarters of the respondents were female (72.7%; $n = 96$), 26.5% ($n = 31$) were male and one respondent preferred not to specify. The overwhelming majority were headteachers (82.6%; $n = 109$), the others were deputy or assistant headteachers (11.4%; $n = 15$), CEOs or Executive Principals (4.5%; $n = 6$) and other (1.5%; $n = 2$). Five of the six CEOs and 60% ($n = 6$) of the deputies/assistants were female. The majority worked in primary schools (62.1%; $n = 82$), 17.4% ($n = 23$) in secondaries, 12.1% ($n = 16$) in first schools, 4.5% ($n = 6$) in middle schools and 3.0% in special schools ($n = 4$). Most secondary leaders (60.9%; $n = 14$) and all special school leaders were male and most primary (80.5%; $n = 66$) and first school (81.3%; $n = 13$) leaders were female. Two-thirds of respondents (67.4%; $n = 89$) were based in local authority-maintained schools (with local support and oversight), a quarter (25.0%; $n = 33$) were based in academies (independent schools funded directly by government); the others regarded themselves as other ($n = 7$) or worked in a pupil referral unit ($n = 1$). The leaders were very experienced. Just over half (51.5%; $n = 68$) had been in post for six years or more and over two-thirds (68.9%; $n = 91$) had been in teaching for between 16 and 30 years.

Of the five headteachers interviewed, two led schools in areas with high levels of disadvantage in one LA (L1 and L3), the middle school leader (L5) had a more mixed catchment in a second LA, and the remaining leaders (L2, L4) worked in more affluent areas in the third, larger LA, which had retained more elements of school support and advice services that many LAs had lost due to national funding cuts after 2010. Two leaders (L1 and L2) were female.

### Data analysis

Due to the relatively small sample, only descriptive and thematic analysis were applied to survey data, differentiating the responses by gender, school type and job role because they were the most relevant to our research questions. Some responses to open questions have also been included. The interview schedule was designed to explore the issues from the survey in more depth and the data that resulted was analyzed using an iterative process of thematic analysis (Boyatzis 1998) to identify recurrent themes, drawing on the theoretical framework for the research and with reference to the survey data. Therefore, this paper is intended to offer a cross-section of contemporaneous views from school leaders in one region of England during the pandemic. Generalisability was not our aim and the findings should regarded as illustrative, rather than representative, of common concerns and issues among school leaders in North East England.

## Findings

### Challenges

The survey began by asking about the greatest challenges leaders had faced in school over the past year, offering them a selection of options derived from the pilot survey. Covid-19 and the lockdown dominated as expected, identified by 91.7% ($n = 121$) of respondents. All CEOs and Executive Principals cited it, along with 95.1% ($n = 78$) of primary-based respondents, but almost half of those who did not cite it (45.4%; $n = 5$) were secondary leaders. After this came funding, cited by almost half of respondents (49.2%; $n = 65$) and national scrutiny from Ofsted or government, which was cited by just over one-third (35.6%; $n = 47$). Male and secondary leaders were over-represented in relation to both these challenges and more than half the deputy or assistant headteachers (60%; $n = 9$) regarded national scrutiny as a challenge. Attendance, exclusion and behaviour issues were cited by one-third of respondents (32.6%; $n = 43$), followed by reductions in social services (31.8%; $n = 42$), parents (28.0%; $n = 37$); morale (25.8%; $n = 34$), local scrutiny (12.1%; $n = 16$) and recruitment, which only 8.3% ($n = 11$) of respondents identified, although this was rather higher in secondaries (17.4%; $n = 4$). In addition, a range of open responses were given, the most common of which related to specific challenges schools faced in relation to special educational needs and disability, English as an additional language needs, falling student numbers, and local issues relating to deprivation or the community.

The five headteachers interviewed were all asked if they agreed with the challenges identified in the survey. Interestingly, while they agreed that the impact of the pandemic was undeniable, finance and funding remained the greatest challenges they faced. In fact,

76        EDUCATIONAL LEADERSHIP AND POLICY IN A TIME OF PRECARITY

Covid-19 had had an intensifying effect: 'the funding and the national scrutiny is actually attached to the pressures that you're trying to cope with COVID' (L3). Two of the leaders referred to 'the relentlessness of the situation', relating to the pressure of having to respond immediately at all times of the day: 'It's that sort of pressure to check emails, to check notifications on a weekend or an evening so you can respond rapidly, so that people can isolate if they need to' (L4). This had had a transformational effect as leaders found themselves with both more to do and new responsibilities. They understood the importance of prioritising safety first for parents and the community as well as in school, but recognised that this was at the expense of other priorities:

> All the things that were [important] to school leaders like academic standards, pastoral care, and wellbeing, yes they were important but they took a backseat to the relentless COVID risk assessment. (L5)

As the same leader emphasised, this had two major consequences. The first was stress, which leaders had both to monitor and mitigate as far as possible. The second was having to respond reactively. He compared this to his experience of trying collectively to turn a failing school around:

> I'd summarise it in the last six months to going back to when we were going through the throes of trying to dig ourselves out of RI [a 'requires improvement' judgement]. Everybody needs a hand. Everybody needs some support. You're plugging your finger in the dyke to stop the holes coming through. It's a bit of a juggling act. (L5)

### Pressure

Leaders were asked to estimate how often on average in the previous year they had found work stressful and felt emotionally drained or exhausted. Just under half (48.8%, $n = 61$) had found work stressful on a daily or almost daily basis and almost one-third (32.0%; $n = 39$) admitted to having felt drained daily or almost daily. Men (59.4%; $n = 19$) were more likely than women (45.7%; $n = 42$) to find work stressful, along with primary leaders (52.6%; $n = 41$) and those from special schools (three of the four surveyed). A similar pattern was detectable in relation to feeling drained daily or almost daily, with male (35.5%; $n = 11$) and primary leaders (35.5%; $n = 27$) again a little more likely to feel this. It was also related to position. More than one-third of headteachers (35.3%; $n = 36$) admitted having felt drained daily or almost daily, compared with only two of the 12 deputies and one of the CEOs. Stress levels had also increased in an overwhelming majority of leaders since the Covid-19 lockdown (85.4%; $n = 105$). Women were more likely to have experienced this (87.9%; $n = 80$) than men (80.6%; $n = 25$) and headteachers (87.5%, $n = 91$), leaders in maintained schools (88.0%; $n = 73$) and primaries (87.0%; $n = 67$) were also more stressed, as were all the special school leaders.

Tellingly, over half the leaders surveyed (54.2%; $n = 71$) said they found it difficult to admit when they felt under pressure. Despite being more likely to find work stressful, men found it slightly harder to admit vulnerability (57.1%; $n = 20$) than women (53.7%; 51). While there was little difference between academies and LA schools, leaders in first schools (68.8%, $n = 11$) and middle schools (66.7%, $n = 4$) found admitting it more difficult than those in primary (51.2%, $n = 42$) or secondary schools (54.5%, $n = 12$). Difficulty also seemed to be associated with leaders' position. Two-thirds of deputy or assistant headteachers (66.7%, $n = 10$) felt this way, compared with just over half the headteachers (55.6%, $n = 60$) and only one of the six CEOs who responded. Asked why, there were 20 open responses about 'keeping up a front' or maintaining a brave face, mostly for colleagues' sakes. Most ominously, one leader stated that they were motivated not to be seen to be struggling 'for fear of what the repercussions that might bring'.

Four of the leaders interviewed initially told us they found it difficult to admit when they felt under pressure. One leader immediately qualified this by saying: 'it's a difficult thing to explain'. He thought he dealt well with stress, partly because, reflecting Howard and Mallory (2008) and others, he was careful to separate work from home:

> I think we all have mechanisms to cope with pressure and stress. I think, for example, at work I have certain colleagues I can say to them, 'Look, I need to talk things through with you' and they to me. That works really well. When I go home, I never want to do that because I also think home has to be home. (L3)

A second leader recognised the complexity of this issue, echoing some of the survey open responses and indicating how the pandemic had again increased the importance of acting as a role model:

> Who do you admit what to as well? I'm quite sure that's the question, isn't it? You don't want to let everybody know that it is particularly difficult at this moment in time because you want your teachers to still think everything's OK (in inverted commas). (L2)

Only one of the leaders had no problem with admitting when they felt under pressure, regarding the modelling issue differently:

> My staff are open about the pressure that they're under and I'm open with them about that pressure that we're all under [...] I think it's by being honest like that that it's much easier to run a school as an organisation where people trust each other and can support each other. I think there's a real danger in the kind of hero headteacher who does everything. I don't think it's a particularly good role model for anybody. (L4)

Reflecting the survey outcomes, the relentless pressure which has already been highlighted was common to all the leaders interviewed, with obvious negative consequences. They identified common issues such as not being able to switch off and agreed that their stress levels had increased because, as well as having to manage their own lives and the needs of children and colleagues, they also had to deal with the growing anxieties of their extended communities: 'Not only are you managing a school with thousands of people connected to it if you include parents, staff, children, you're also managing your own life' (L1). Even the headteacher who did not feel his personal stress levels had increased agreed that lockdown has created new difficulties: 'Headteachers have always been pulled in every direction but I think that there's an increased pressure with that at the moment' (L4).

### *Support*

The survey then asked where leaders go for support in relation to challenges they face in school and when they feel stressed or exhausted. Logically they were most likely to turn to colleagues in school in response to challenges there. Just over half (53.8%; $n = 71$) did this, including five of the six CEOs. Leaders in maintained schools were more likely to do so (57.3%; $n = 51$) than in academies and those in secondaries (60.9%; $n = 14$) more than in other school types. After this came colleagues in other schools (50.0%; 66), where leaders in maintained schools (59.6%; $n = 53$) and female leaders (56.3%; $n = 54$) were over-represented. After this, they went to governors (36.4%; 48); family/friends (28.8%; $n = 37$); colleagues in their LA or multi-academy trust (22.0%; 29); and local professional networks (22.0%; 29). Fewer than 15% of leaders went to their line manager or more distant professional networks on school-based issues.

There was a different picture in relation to who they went to when they felt stressed or exhausted. Most strikingly, over one-third of leaders (34.1%; $n = 45$) indicated that they drew on none of the options for support. This group included half of the CEOs; almost half of academy leaders (48.5%; $n = 16$) and deputy/assistant heads (46.7%; $n = 7$); 43.5% ($n = 10$) of secondary leaders ($n = 10$) and 40% of male leaders. Family and friends were the most important among those who responded, selected by 42.4% ($n = 56$) of leaders. Male leaders (34.3%, $n = 12$) and CEOs (only one of the six in the sample) were less likely to turn to them. Leaders were much less likely to consult colleagues either in school (20.5%; $n = 27$) or from other schools (15.2%; $n = 20$) when stressed. All other options, which included professional networks, line managers and doctors/therapists were identified by 6% or fewer of respondents.

All the leaders interviewed had strong informal networks with local leaders. This was an important release valve and a means of validating the experiences of all of the leaders interviewed. One combined an informal WhatsApp group with local middle school leaders with support from a group of longstanding friends who had also become headteachers, two based in other countries. However, the amount of formal support they received from their LA varied. The two leaders in the largest of the three LAs appreciated the amount of support available. In contrast, one of the leaders in a smaller LA, which also had the highest levels of disadvantage, highlighted 'the disparity between the support you get as a maintained school and the support you get if you're part of a MAT' (L1). She felt its small size also restricted the amount of formal support she was able to draw on from local leaders because 'People know too much. You can't be honest' (L1), although the other leader based in the LA saw this more positively as the basis of a collaborative approach.

### Access to regular support/supervision

Three-quarters of the leaders surveyed would welcome access to regular support like the supervision offered to clinical professionals (74.4%; $n = 87$). This was most important to CEOs, male leaders and secondary leaders, all of which were overlapping groups, perhaps because they had fewer other support options. Four of the headteachers interviewed addressed this issue. One thought it was a good idea in principle 'but would you want to access it?' (L3). Another also thought it would bring benefits, especially for new headteachers, and a third had explored the idea but it had never progressed. Only one of the leaders interviewed had experienced such support, which his school had offered. He was clear about the benefits:

> At the back of the summer term I accessed some counselling, six hour [long] sessions, [...] because at that point there I was probably feeling a little bit sort of short-tempered and a bit

agitated […] Sometimes I carry a little bit of that baggage home. And so for that reason I accessed a little bit of counselling just to say, 'Well, this is the sort of stuff I'm contending with', and it was really good to get an impartial point of view. (L5)

## Autonomy

As already indicated, the survey also asked about autonomy, one of the factors central to school self-improvement policy. More than half of respondents who answered the question felt either very autonomous (17.8%; $n = 21$) or autonomous (36.4%; $n = 43$). Female leaders were more likely to feel very autonomous (20.7%; $n = 18$) than male leaders (10.0%; $n = 3$). Leaders in maintained schools (58.8%; $n = 47$) and primary schools (56.8%; $n = 42$) were more likely to feel autonomous or very autonomous than those in academies (32.1%; $n = 9$) or secondaries (42.9%; $n = 9$). However, given the amount of pressures they also stated they faced, autonomy did not appear to be a supportive factor (Thompson, Lingard, and Ball 2020). We also explored the leaders interviewed how autonomous they felt in the professional decisions they made. The leader who felt 'completely autonomous' had moved from leading an academy to a mainstream primary school, reflecting the survey outcomes, although pressure was created by the fact that 'you have to make the decisions yourself' (L1). While two of the other leaders spoke of feeling 'well-supported' in school, particularly by their governors, another feared what we might call 'responsibility creep':

> There are a lot of decisions that you make, more and more and more within this job, that are so far away from children and education. From building work, from drainage, from cyclical maintenance to which support agency you go to. It never stops to be honest. (L3)

Alongside financial constraints, he felt it was external factors, which the pandemic had intensified, that prevented him from taking some decisions, rather than lack of autonomy.

## Rethinking schools

Finally, the survey asked how leaders could or should rethink schools in the light of the lockdown experience, selecting from the outcomes of the pilot survey. The most popular response was to have more trust in schools and reduce accountability pressures, which was selected by three-quarters of leaders (75.0%; $n = 99$). Responses varied according to the gender and phase of the leaders. Female (79.2%; ($n = 76$) and primary leaders (81.7%; $n = 67$) were more likely to select this than male (62.9%; $n = 22$) and secondary (65.2%; $n = 15$) leaders. However, only 68.8% ($n = 11$) of first school leaders selected this. After this came mental health issues. Focusing more on the mental health and well-being of children and young people was selected by half the leaders (50.8%; $n = 67$) selected. Again, a difference could be seen between female (53.1%; $n = 15$) and primary (52.4%; $n = 43$) leaders, compared with male 42.3% ($n = 15$) and secondary leaders 43.5% ($n = 10$). This was also the case with focusing more on the mental health and well-being of adults in schools, selected by 47.7% ($n = 63$) of leaders. More than half the female (51.0%; $n = 49$) and primary (52.4%; $n = 43$) leaders selected this, compared with 47.8% ($n = 11$) of secondary and 37.1% ($n = 13$) of male leaders. Maintained school leaders regarded both issues as more important than academy leaders. The other issues cited were broadening the curriculum (33.3%; $n = 44$); rethinking schools' role in safeguarding/social care (25.8%; $n = 34$); changing the structure of the school day/term (25.0%; $n = 33$); offering more online training/teaching (17.4%; $n = 23$); and working with parents (16.7%; $n = 22$).

We also highlight two issues which emerged when the leaders interviewed were asked how far lockdown represented an opportunity to rethink schools: accountability and technology-influenced change.

### Rethinking accountability

Accountability was the primary theme that emerged from the interviews and the responses offered a nuanced picture of the issues involved. All the leaders felt that it was both necessary and useful, particularly in managing the transition into secondary school, but that the current approach was too crude and divisive. The following observation was fairly typical:

> It's the publishing of data I think [that] causes a lot of stress and anxiety for schools, particularly because I've always worked in [disadvantaged] schools like this. And you always do the best by the children. And you shouldn't be feeling that you're not doing a good enough job just because the school down the road gets better results than you. (L1)

Concerns were also expressed about the effectiveness of high stakes assessment: 'What does testing actually do?' (L3). A second leader was adamant that the pandemic had revealed both that schools' resilience and that accountability structures are not sacrosanct:

> In terms of accountability as well, have schools fallen apart without this sort of punitive inspection regime? No, they've risen to the challenge and are doing a really really good job. (L4)

Another of the leaders hoped for assessment to be rethought to focus more on children's learning: 'something which I think is a little bit more forensic [...] to help the children learn in the future' (L5). Although one of the leaders regretted the negative effect on children of what he called the time wasted 'finely tuning' them for SATs, mental health was not an issue which they identified in relation to rethinking schools, perhaps because it had been discussed (in relation to themselves) in other aspects of the interviews.

### Technology supporting change

The use of technology was the second theme that emerged, although more in relation to instigating new ways of working than to training (which only one leader emphasised) and teaching, which may explain why the survey did not highlight the latter issues so strongly. One of the leaders was representative in suggesting that the necessity of doing things differently had 'given us a chance to explore things that we wouldn't normally choose to explore' (L2). This included improving children's digital skills, but also how they communicate with parents:

> I think communication is key. I think sometimes in our communication systems, we just hold on to things that are archaic. [...] The government, the Department of Education, Ofsted, the first thing they look at is your website. I think the response [in a parent

EDUCATIONAL LEADERSHIP AND POLICY IN A TIME OF PRECARITY 81

survey] was about 2% of my parents actually bothered to look at that. The mobile messages or the Facebook information page – [they are] perfect for sharing information. (L3)

In another school they were running assemblies on Zoom and no longer sending letters home but communicating with parents entirely through other media. A survey of parents had also revealed that every family had access to smartphones, which allowed them to use that technology, supplemented by DfE-supplied laptops loaned to families with book-marks already set up with books for all the websites children needed. In such ways schools were able to overcome the barriers to learning created by the pandemic.

## Conclusion

It is hardly surprising that during a period when Covid-19 has increased leaders' sense of vulnerability by closing schools and creating concerns about the long-term educational and social effects on children and young people (Van Lancker and Parolin 2020), the overwhelming majority of leaders in our survey included it among the greatest challenges they had faced in the previous year. What is more surprising is that leaders interviewed felt that, rather than being overwhelming in itself, the pandemic had had an amplifying effect on the greatest challenges they faced, which remained finance and accountability. As one leader stated tellingly, 'These things that are happening at the moment are less stressful than leading a school in special measures'. Our analysis also reveals that the pan-demic has presented leaders with huge pressures through 'responsibility creep' in the areas of health and safeguarding. More than eight out of ten leaders surveyed felt their stress levels had increased since the lockdown. Gender seems to have an effect in how leaders respond. Male leaders (many of whom were also secondary leaders) were more likely to feel stressed and exhausted regularly, unlike in Tahir et al.'s (2017) study, and were less likely to admit it. They were also more likely to welcome counselling support. However, female leaders were more likely both to see the pandemic as a chal-lenge and to associate it with increased stress. There were also differences according to position. Headteachers were more likely to feel drained and deputies/assistants less likely to admit feeling under pressure. This suggests that differentiated levels of targeted support needs to be available to these groups. The views of the leaders interviewed (none of whom were based in secondaries) did not obviously vary by gender or their commu-nities' degree of disadvantage, and they all spoke of the need to remain resilient and support colleagues, children and their communities. Although leaders surveyed perhaps surprisingly felt they did not lack autonomy, albeit less so among secondary and academy leaders, the experiences of those interviewed suggest that the pandemic reduced the energy and agency that Steward (2014) asserts are essential to build leaders' emotional resilience.

In terms of whom they go to for support, our second research question, leaders had a range of sources and were understandably most likely to turn to colleagues in relation to challenges in school. The picture was less reassuring in relation to feeling stressed or exhausted. A third of leaders surveyed stated they had no sources of support in this respect, a proportion that was higher among CEOs, deputies, male and academy leaders. Although none of the leaders interviewed felt they were in this position, the fact that only one of them had had the opportunity to access any kind of counselling or supervision and that three-quarters of the leaders surveyed would welcome this kind of support suggests that this is an area that needs serious consideration. It also reveals that little progress has been made in relation to the kinds of emotional support Beatty (2000), Crawford (2007) and others were calling for more than a decade ago. Male leaders seem a particular concern, although the relatively low numbers in the research underline that this is an area for further exploration. This is where a recalibration of vulnerability, reinforced by professional support, could have a real effect. One of the leaders interviewed explicitly identified the fact that the isolation of the pandemic had underlined to her and her colleagues the importance of attending to their 'emotional wellbeing' as a group and like other participants, felt that the challenges of the pandemic had increased trust in their schools and their communities, one of Ruck Simmonds' (2009) characteristics of critical vulnerability. However, the upheaval and uncertainty created by the pandemic seems to have denied leaders the space to focus on the other key elements such as risk-taking, creativity and intense self-reflection and follow Kelchtermans (2005) in really 'embracing' their sense of vulnerability.

Trust was also the issue that emerged most strongly in relation to the final research question, how can this knowledge be used to rethink how schools work? Three-quarters of leaders wanted more trust in schools, which recent research suggests has been eroding for some time (Stone-Johnson and Miles Weiner 2020), and less emphasis on accountability. Related to this, they also wanted more focus on supporting the mental health and wellbeing of both children and adults in schools. The leaders interviewed were clear that this did not mean abandoning accountability but building on the trust placed on them in looking after 'vulnerable' and keyworker children during the pandemic. It was also of note that the emphasis in the interviews on technology related to it being used to increase flexibility and effect change. However, along with leaders' reluctance to admit weakness, the lack of trust they identified at system level and lack of emphasis on wellbeing seem likely to prevent the development of the kind of critical vulnerability that might help them deal with, and reduce, the stress they experience.

The limitations of the research relate to its relatively small sample, the necessary use of online interviews, the relative under-representation of secondary schools and its focus on one English region. Further research is needed to explore key issues around pressure, lack of support and trust, and variations according to gender, position and school type that the pandemic has amplified. More research is also needed into the impact and human cost of pressure and precarity on school leaders, as well as into the potential for vulnerability to be regarded more positively. It is to be hoped that as schools emerge from the pandemic, leaders can use the lack of restriction as an opportunity to stimulate change and draw on the sense of vulnerability that we have all gained through it more profitably.

## Disclosure statement

No potential conflict of interest was reported by the author(s).

## References

Angel, K. 2021. *Tomorrow Sex Will be Good Again*. London: Verso.

Ball, S. 2017. *The Education Debate*. 3rd ed. Bristol: Policy Press.

Beatty, B. R. 2000. "The Emotions of Educational Leadership: Breaking the Silence." *International Journal Leadership in Education* 3 (4): 331–357.

Berkovich, I., and O. Eyal. 2015. "Educational Leaders and Emotions: An International Review of Empirical Evidence 1992–2012." *Review of Educational Research* 85 (1): 129–167.

Boyatzis, R. E. 1998. *Transforming Qualitative Information: Thematic Analysis and Code Development*. Thousand Oaks, CA: SAGE.

Bullough, R. V. 2005. "Teacher Vulnerability and Teachability: A Case Study of a Mentor and two Interns." *Teacher Education Quality* 32 (2): 23–39.

Bullough, R. V. 2019. *Essays on Teaching Education and the Inner Drama of Teaching*. Emerald: Bingley.

Bush, T. 2011. "Succession Planning in England: New Leaders and new Forms of Leadership." *School Leadership and Management* 31 (3): 181–198.

Crawford, M. 2007. "Rationality and Emotion in Primary School Leadership: an Exploration of Key Themes." *Educational Review* 59 (1): 87–98.

Dale, M., and E. M. Frye. 2009. "Vulnerability and the Love of Learning as Necessities for Wise Teacher Education." *Journal of Teacher Education* 60: 123–130.

DfE. 2010. *The Importance of Teaching*. London: DfE.

Dussault, M., and S. Thibodeau. 1997. "Professional Isolation and Performance at Work of School Principals." *Journal of School Leadership* 7: 521–536.

Ecclestone, K., and D. Hayes. 2019. *The Dangerous Rise of Therapeutic Education*. 2nd ed. London: Routledge.

Ecclestone, K., and C. Rawdin. 2016. "Reinforcing the 'Diminished' Subject? The Implications of the 'Vulnerability Zeitgeist' for Well-Being in Educational Settings." *Cambridge Journal of Education* 46 (3): 377–393.

Ginsberg, R., and T. Gray Davies. 2003. "The Emotional Side of Leadership." In *Effective Educational Leadership*, edited by N. Bennett, M. Crawford, and M. Cartwright, 267–280. Trowbridge: The Open University/Paul Chapman Publishing.

Greany, T., and R. Higham. 2018. *Hierarchy, Markets and Networks: Analysing the 'Self-Improving School-led System' Agenda in England and the Implications for Schools*. London: UCL IOE Press.

Hadfield, M., and M. Ainscow. 2018. "Inside a Self-Improving System: Collaboration, Competition and Transition." *Journal of Educational Change* 19: 441–462.

Hargreaves, D. H. 2010. *Creating a Self-Improving System*. Nottingham: NCSL.

Howard, M. P., and B. J. Mallory. 2008. "Perceptions of Isolation among High School Principals." *Journal of Women in Educational Leadership* 6 (1): 7–27.

Huber, S. G., and C. Helm. 2020. "COVID-19 and Schooling: Evaluation, Assessment and Accountability in Times of Crises." *Educational Assessment, Evaluation and Accountability* 32: 237–270.

Izgar, H. 2009. "An Investigation of Depression and Loneliness among School Principals." *Educational Sciences: Theory and Practice* 9 (1): 247–258.

Jones, R. 1994. "The Loneliness of Leadership." *The Executive Educator* 16 (3): 26–30.

Jopling, M. 2018. "Is There a North-South Divide Between Schools in England?" *Management in Education* 33 (1): 37–40.

Kelchtermans, G. 1996. "Teacher Vulnerability: Understanding its Moral and Political Roots." *Cambridge Journal of Education* 26 (3): 307–323.

Kelchtermans, G. 2005. "Teachers' Emotions in Educational Reforms: Self-Understanding, Vulnerable Commitment and Micropolitical Literacy." *Teaching and Teacher Education* 21: 995–1006.

Kelchtermans, G., L. Piot, and K. Ballet. 2011. "The Lucid Loneliness of the Gatekeeper: Exploring the Emotional Dimension in Principals' Work Lives." *Oxford Review of Education* 37 (1): 93–108.

Morrison, M., and K. Ecclestone. 2011. "Getting Emotional: A Critical Evaluation of Recent Trends in the Development of School Leaders." *School Leadership and Management* 31 (3): 199–214.

NAHT. 2019. *About Time: Life as a Middle Leader.* Haywards Heath: NAHT.

Potter, T., and G. Brotherton. 2013. "What Do We Mean When We Talk about 'Vulnerability?'" In *Working with Vulnerable Children, Young People and Families*, edited by G. Brotherton and M. Cronin, 1–15. London: Routledge.

Ruck Simmonds, M. 2009. "Critical Vulnerability: An Imperative Approach to Educational Leadership." *Journal of Thought* 42 (1/2): 79–97.

Salvatore, J., and J. McVarish. 2014. "Vulnerability: A Metalogue." *Counterpoints* 380: 47–59.

Simkins, T., J. Coldron, M. Crawford, and B. Maxwell. 2018. "Emerging Schooling Landscapes in England: How Primary System Leaders are Responding to New School Groupings." *Education Management Administration and Leadership* 47 (3): 3311–3348.

Stephenson, L., and S. Bauer. 2010. "The Role of Isolation in Predicting new Principals' Burnout." *International Journal of Education Policy and Leadership* 5 (9): 1–17.

Steward, J. 2014. "Sustaining Emotional Resilience for School Leadership." *School Leadership & Management* 34 (1): 52–68.

Stone-Johnson, C., and J. Miles Weiner. 2020. "Principal Professionalism in the Time of COVID-19." *Journal of Professional Capital and Community* 5 (3/4): 367–374.

Tahir, L., M. Thakib, M. Hamzah, M. Said, and M. Musah. 2017. "Novice Head Teachers' Isolation and Loneliness Experiences: A Mixed-Methods Study." *Educational Management Administration & Leadership* 45 (1): 164–189.

Thompson, G., B. Lingard, and S. J. Ball. 2020. "'Indentured Autonomy': Headteachers and Academisation Policy in Northern England." *Journal of Educational Administration and History*: 53 (3-4): 215–232.

Van Lancker, W., and Z. Parolin. 2020. "COVID-19, School Closures, and Child Poverty: A Social Crisis in the Making." *The Lancet* 5 (5): 243–244.

Zorn, D., and M. Boler. 2007. "Rethinking Emotions and Educational Leadership." *International Journal of Leadership in Education* 10 (2): 137–151.

# Repositioned professionals and heterodox: a response to the precarity of reform in further education

Lewis Entwistle

**ABSTRACT**
The precarity of professionals working in schools and colleges at a time of change has been strongly accented by the competitive markets that currently characterise education and the influence of its global reforms. In this article, I draw on empirical data from a project located in a sixth-form college to argue that the field of Further Education is being restructured such that professionalism is hollowed out whilst accountability measures undermine leaders' authority and enable a low-trust culture. I use Bourdieu's thinking tools to conceptualise the data, including a rich conceptualisation of this site as a 'field' and of practices within it as part of the 'game in play'. I generate four metaphorical lenses through which a perception of heterodoxy is used to clarify alternative positions that are simultaneously adopted by players and from which a response to the changing field of education reform can be offered.

## Introduction

Contemporary critical debates that theorise around state education precarity point to the repositioning of professionals within newly competitive markets as an indication of creeping privatisations, growing commodification of the public sphere and the rise of the global education reform movement (GERM). I argue that the restructuring forces that drive professionals into uncomfortable, simultaneously held positions can offer a positive response to a low-trust organisation culture.

The study recounted here discusses the details of a project called the Hillvale Project. Firstly it examined the way staff working in the Further Education (FE) sector in England tried to find a way of responding to their sense of precarity, redressing what Peters (2017) describes as the diminishing of the professional standing of workers wounded by the neoliberal state, its 'empowerment of consumers' (142) and the morality of consumerism. I present key findings and introduce Bourdieu's formulations of the heterodox, a manifestation of opposites and possibles, as an innovative contribution to the critical debate.

Secondly, the Hillvale project applies four metaphorical and reflexive lenses following Bourdieu's (1984) game-player metaphor. A condition of reflexivity is, according to Bourdieu (1998) 'not only to invent responses, but to invent a way of inventing responses, to invent new forms of organisation, of the work of contestation, of the task of activism'

(58). As such, the lenses question the *doxa*, which is the taken-for-granted positioning embedded in the field structured by GERM. I consider here to what extent a heterodoxic reply from professionals can create a potential space to 'speak back' to the orthodoxy of the field (Bourdieu 1994, Fitzgerald 2008; Apple 2013).

The paper is organised firstly to consider policy concerns and global reforms that have driven a community of repositioned professionals to feel precarious and vulnerable. From here the paper establishes the context of metaphor as an established methodological approach and to include Bourdieu's work. The paper then introduces the Hillvale project before working through the metaphorical lenses as a series to prompt discussion, before augmenting the case for the heterodox.

## Global education reform

The global power of GERM generates a crisis of professional confidence (Choudry and Williams 2017) on the one hand and the necessary compliance of operatives (Dow et al. 2000; Hall and McGinity 2015) on the other. Managers learn to categorise competencies through teaching standards and teacher effectiveness programmes which translate the reach and penetration of the reform agenda into data (Ceulemans, Maarten, and Struyf 2012; Page 2017). Underpinned thus by ever-increasing policy technologies (Ball 2006), GERM makes explicit the requirements of a performative society. Whilst such performance regimes may at first imply a position of organisational power (Fitzgerald 2008; Courtney and Gunter 2015), they in fact operate strategies of surveillance and control through their increased instrumentality (Gewirtz and Ball 2000; Foster 2004; Newman 2004) which in turn produces a growing sense of professional powerlessness, alienation and exclusion (Smyth 2011). Subsequently, the tools measuring policy reach contribute to worsening working conditions (Apple 2011) and an intensification of workloads, a sense of human utility (Casey 2003), and, it may be argued, a totalitarian control over the field of education (Fielding 2006). In consequence, education is reinvented as a failing system and teachers are recast as the agents of that failure that in turn strengthens the growth of a global education orthodoxy (Fuller and Stevenson 2019).

Often fuelled by the short-term thinking of governments who want to see 'results' improve during their term in office, a plethora of reforms have captured the professional focus of education through the utility of a 'new managerialism' (Hartley 1997; Pollitt 2014). Over time professionals situated within the organisation have been re-cultured towards entrepreneurialism (Hall, Gunter, and Bragg 2012; Gunter and Hall 2013), corporatism (Courtney 2015) and the acquisition of technical rationalities (Newman 2005). They find themselves repositioned towards policy enactment (Rayner and Gunter 2020) by the endless cycles and uncertainties of policy change which have increasingly complicated the current system and often fail to deliver the improvements they were designed to achieve (Barker 2008).

Education reforms have encouraged acceptance of those conditions evidently responsible for complex professional precarity, job insecurity and contradictory positioning (see Rayner and Gunter 2020). Through de-professionalisation and dismantling of an occupational community, and as a consequence of a market in human capital which prefers the expert of celebrity teachers, gurus and tzars, the repositioning of professionals upon a field of permanent reinvention has reduced their practices to that of the technician

(Bourdieu 1998, Casey 2003; Standing 2011). As such, the contemporary realities of work in the field of education, and specifically the FE sector gravitates towards activities of evidence-collecting, value-accrediting and, through associated performance-measurement technologies, accumulating data. Indeed, the pervasive effect of recent austerity policies has encouraged a growing individualisation of professional work in which the accelerated shrinking of resources and improved efficiencies of increasingly unaffordable systems (Smyth 2011) legitimises instability, policy churn and change.

The ensuing creep of vulnerability into previously secure sectors is a politically induced sense of impermanence (Bottery 2000; Butler 2016; Lazar and Sanchez 2019) a 'destructuring of existence' (Bourdieu 1998, 82), and depoliticisation of both public service and professional discourse (Courtney and McGinity 2020). Standing (2011) discusses the negative social impact and disintegration of work communities through unlimited labour flexibility, or as Bourdieu (1998) describes it 'flexploitation' (85) and Ozga and Lawn's (1988) remark that we are witnessing the proletarianisation of the teaching profession is taken up by others pursuing the critical debate (Courtney and Gunter 2015 ; Hardy 2015; Hughes, Gunter, and Courtney 2019) in addressing the neutralising of professional voices, the required adoption of espoused values, purposes and ideologies, and the disposability of professional experience as unwanted human capital. Individual workers within the organisation have become responsibilised (Bourdieu 1998; Peters 2017) into adapting and transforming towards new accountabilities, fragilities or demonstrations of innovative expertise and entrepreneurialism in order to keep their jobs.

Therefore, critical discourse circulates around issues of conspicuous professional practice, of performativity, of professional accountabilities, of coercive management controls, corporatism and of the outsourcing of services, and the commercialisation of teaching products (Ball 2006, 2008; Courtney 2015; Gulson et al. 2017; Lingard et al. 2017; Page 2017; Greany and Higham 2018; Skerritt 2019). Reductionist and oversimplified understandings of education (Gardner 2019) have gathered momentum and changed public discourse, reshaping our thinking on what education is and who controls it (Riddle and Apple 2019). GERM as a manifestation of neoliberal globalisation replicates the social order of capitalism through incessant revolutions, constant reorganisation, merger and fragmentation, (Hardy 2015). Bourdieu (1990) defines this condition as the logic of economic practice, as evidenced in the FE 'market', and can be interpreted as a symbolic violence of domination against those concerned with the core values of education: relational and process-driven encounters with 'people, things and events' (Greenfield 1993, 21).

## Metaphors

To interrogate and conceptualise the project's findings I construct metaphors. Metaphor, as a conceptual research tool is an established methodological approach in understanding complicated organisational phenomena (Cornellissen 2005). In choosing to work with metaphors I am following this tradition, developing what Greenfield (1993) calls an 'understanding (that) comes from setting the images against each other' (71), and exposing frictions within the data. Metaphors have generative potential (Schon 1993), fulfil a heuristic role (Weick 1989) and change our perceptions through metaphoric discourse

(Ricoeur 1978). As vehicles of sense-making, metaphors operate as creative catalysts in organisational theory building. As a platform of academic inquiry, Boxenbaum and Rouleau (2011) recommend a wide range of metaphors from which new theories form, producing images that stimulate imaginative responses and which enable theorists to generate novel perspectives on organisational life. Metaphor, as a common and accepted way of communicating, is a powerful interpretative vehicle (Greenfield 1993), and offers both critical and creative perspectives, (Alvesson and Spicer 2016). The metaphors used in the project are dependent upon each other, are generative tools, and energise the dynamics of the field.

Current academic work in this area and recorded recently in this journal (see special issue, Heffernan, Netolicky, and Mockler 2019), espouses the vitality of metaphor as a structural framework for thinking through complex and abstract phemomena. Drawing on a rich and-wide ranging theoretical tradition, metaphor therefore constructs frameworks, conceptualisations, classifications and interpretations that can often clarify the messy, abstract and fluid reality of data (Lakoff and Johnson 2003; Flusberg, Teenie Matlock, and Thibodeau 2018; Heffernan 2019; Netolicky 2019; Samier 2019). Usefully, Ortenblad, Putnam, and Trehan (2016) encourage the generating of new metaphors through evaluation, critique, empirical or experiential observations, fantasy, and conceptual development. Maguire and Braun (2019) and Schechter et al. (2018) deconstruct dominant narratives, and Rayner and Gunter (2020) explore position-taking.

Similarly, Bourdieu's metaphor of games and game-playing articulates positions on a field as a social space. Bourdieu (1993) describes the field as a place of 'forces' and 'struggles' (10) which both transform and conserve, through a network, the objective positions strategically adopted by those occupying the field. These positions can be defended or improved but are determined and defined by 'the space of possibles' (Bourdieu 1993, 10) and constitute the particulars of the field in a constantly changing 'universe of options' (10). An environment of fluctuating position-taking but finite strategies and meanings is produced (Ferrare and Apple 2015). The field is an arena where objective relations are negotiated through the fluid positions on offer. These positions are not evenly distributed, often hierarchical, and are occupied by institutions or people/ agents (Thomson 2017) through their investment of capital which can be social, economic, cultural/symbolic. The capital produced has a reflexive dynamic which 'only reproduces its effects upon the field in which it is produced and reproduced' (Bourdieu 1984, 107). The power and symbolic order of the field is maintained through orthodoxy, but its *doxa* and *illusio* is challenged and subverted by sustained heterodoxy.

The *doxa* is a claimed position on the field demanding the tacit acceptance of impositions and sanctions which, through practice, protects the nature of the game and preserves the continuity of the field through compliance (Bourdieu 1990). The *illusio* is that which presupposes the necessity of the game whilst determining the investment of the players' interest in it. Both *doxa* and *illusio* protect the established positions of powerful players on the field. Heterodoxy challenges the orthodoxy of the game on the field and also its *doxa* (Choudry and Williams 2017). Heterodoxy therefore makes explicit the sum total of opposites (Bourdieu 1994) from which choices become apparent and many further possibles emerge. As a sustained challenge, refusing to play the game on the field and questioning what is at stake in the wider field (Choudry and Williams 2017), heterodoxy facilitates a critical discourse by destroying the false self-evidences

EDUCATIONAL LEADERSHIP AND POLICY IN A TIME OF PRECARITY      89

of orthodoxy, and avoiding a fictitious restoration of *doxa* (Bottero 2009). Bourdieu's metaphors help in explaining how professional repositioning, as a lived-through experience of those working in one FE institution, can be theorised.

## About the project

### Sixth form colleges

The Hillvale Project was located in one organisation within a discreet sector of FE, a sixth-form college (referred to subsequently as SFC). Although caricatured as exam factories (Hodkinson and Bloomer 2000), SFCs and 16–19 academies represent a broadening sector educating over 152,000 students. According to the Sixth-Form Colleges Association (2020) there are currently 78 SFCs and 16–19 academies, 1453 academy sixth forms and 399 school sixth-forms in the state sector indicative of the quasi-markets (Ball 2008; Riddle and Apple 2019) of education provision across England. They are gathered in regional clusters, rather than uniformly spread across the country; a vestige of comprehensivisation, interpreted differently by local education authorities in England in the 1960s and 1970s (Shorter 1994).

SFCs and FE colleges became independent of their local education authorities following the 1992 Further and Higher Education Act, in a process known as 'incorporation' (Robinson and Burke 1996). The Act marked a reform of post-16 education towards modernisation policies designed to improve the performance of the post-16 sector (Lumby 2003a). College principals became autonomous chief executives of their self-managing organisations, but in replacing local democratic control with independent management status, the Act introduced aggressive market conditions into the sector, controlling their autonomy with relentless central government policy-making (Ball 1993; Lumby 2003b Barker 2008; Smyth 2011; Stoten 2014; McGinity 2015).

The consequences of the 1992 Act have since isolated and fragmented the sector (Stoten 2014). Competing against 'rival' organisations has become a precondition of the work of SFCs. Regressive funding mechanisms have proved powerful structural pressures and an effective controlling tool (Briggs 2004). By rationing resources and materials, central government policy has sought to control a post 16 market through disruptive reconfigurations. The public scrutiny of the yearly examination cycle for enrolled students (Lumby 2003a) and the application of national standards by a government franchised inspection regime – OFSTED successfully weaves precarity into the sector through increased competition and high-risk consequences within and between institutions.

### The case study

The ontological position from which my project grew assumes that organisations are sites of communicative action initiated by people gathered in a social ensemble (Casey 2002) and as social organisations are constructed from the people within it (Greenfield 1993). The project drew on the close participation of 17 colleagues from across all sectors of one medium-sized SFC, Hillvale College. Seven members (Table 1) were associated with a loosely structured staff group, called an engagement group, working collaboratively on some 20 planned 'staff participatory events' over an 18-month period.

EDUCATIONAL LEADERSHIP AND POLICY IN A TIME OF PRECARITY

**Table 1.** Research participants from the engagement group.

| Participant | College role | 5 years + at Hillvale |
| --- | --- | --- |
| 1 | Teacher | Yes |
| 2 | Teacher | No |
| 3 | Support | No |
| 4 | Director + support | Yes |
| 5 | Support | Yes |
| 6 | Teacher (+chair) | No |
| 7 | Support | Yes |

The second group of six research participants was recruited from the senior leadership team (Table 2), as an 'instance' that could yield contrasting data to that collected from engagement group participants.

The third group of four participants (Table 3) was recruited from colleagues who had responded to a consultation project administered by the engagement group.

The balance between male and female employees, between support and teaching employees and between time served at the college is not a 'scientifically' accurate reflection of the demography of the college but represents a useful cross section of the population from which a workable participant sample could be taken. The three sample respondent groups were therefore typical of the organisation's structure (Merkens 2004) with representatives recruited from those various communities working at Hillvale College.

Nineteen semi-structured interviews were transcribed and coded thematically against emergent patterns and utterances before comparative work was done across the accumulating data; a process described by Boulton and Hammersley (2006) as mutually fitting across data and categories. Seven participants were asked to complete image-work as part of the interviews, a process similar to concept mapping recommended by Mavers, Somekh, and Restorick (2002) as a tool to provoke and sustain discussion. Five written journals were submitted from engagement group members recording attitudes and feelings about the group's activities, perception of their own work and reflections on professional practice. According to Gibson and Brown (2009), the use of unstructured journals help 'to iteratively develop the themes of analysis from the data rather than trying to pre-specify them' (78).

I also recorded my observations throughout the project in a research dairy. These were of two types: that of participant observer working with the engagement group as 'the research instrument' (Yin 2016) recording events as they happen, and that of reflective observer recording recollections and remembrances of practices that occur after the event.

Understanding the data that emerged from my interaction with the study's participants is a reflexive process involving structure and agency. I followed the premise that

**Table 2.** Research participants from the senior leadership team.

| Name | College role | 5 years+ at Hillvale |
| --- | --- | --- |
| 8 | Associate Director | Yes |
| 9 | Director | Yes |
| 10 | Associate Director | Yes |
| 11 | Associate Director | Yes |
| 12 | Principal | Yes |
| 13* | Director | Yes |

* also CEG member.

**Table 3.** Research participants from college staff.

| Name | College role | 5 years+ at Hillvale |
|---|---|---|
| 14 | Support | Yes |
| 15 | Teacher | Yes |
| 16 | Teacher | Yes |
| 17 | Teacher | Yes |

if the engagement group is a product of the culture of Hillvale, so those investing 'capital' in it (members, SLT, other staff) do so as producers whose interests reveal the state of the field of production. The producers are involved in positioning and position-taking on the field and are positioned by it at the same time. Evidence from the fieldwork was transformed into qualitative data and thematically categorised using Bourdieu's field theory, game-playing, and thinking tools of capitals and agency.

## The metaphorical lenses

My four metaphorical lenses each contain its own pattern of logic that catches the symbolic nature of indeterminate and fuzzy utterances (Bourdieu 1990) that consists of the thoughts, feelings and opinions of the study's participants as co-authors of narratives. To explain what is structuring the field of cultural production at Hillvale and the cultural practices of those players situated on, or in proximity to the field the Lock and Key, the Welcome Mat, the Mantelpiece and the Cuckoo interpret various games in play.

### The Lock and Key

The Lock and Key lens establishes and protects taken-for-granted rules of the game, the *doxa*. It represents the conserving activities that many colleges find themselves undertaking. If FE is in a 'crisis' (Hall and McGinity 2015) the Lock and Key lens exercises gatekeeping characteristics to mitigate against threats. A positivist rendition of organisational power through what is accountable and measurable (Gray and Jenkins 1993; Fielding 2001; Newman 2004; Gunter 2016) replenishes traditional hierarchy and helps to define cultures of efficiency and effectiveness that can in turn be interpreted as sensible and rational (Apple 2008). Accordingly, it could be suggested that those organisational members who have acquired power, are inclined to protect their capital possession of it (Eacott 2013) and rarely relinquish it, unless to improve self-interested domination of the field of organisational power (Michels 1915; cited in Casey 2002). Conversely, a parallel culture of deselection, of blame, and of learnt subordination that reinforces a sense of 'unworthiness' (Bourdieu 1998, 99) complicates the metaphor of the Lock and Key and the associated organisational traits of a trustless organisation (Fielding 2006), one demanding compliant enforcement of the *doxa*.

### The Welcome Mat

The Welcome Mat lens amplifies orthodoxy whilst passing over a threshold. It forms relations and builds a trusting organisation (Hartley 2010). In moving towards what Gergen (2003) describes as participatory democratic practice, and what Townsend

(2013) suggests is the potential to achieve socially just aims, the warming sensitivities of the Welcome Mat can potentially energise the organisation through therapeutic and affective community practices. According to Fielding (2001) such communities offer a sentimental standpoint and, whilst championing the personal, may offer resistance to the hierarchic and trustless functions, as defined by the Lock and Key. Through interpersonal orientations, Fielding (2006) points to an 'inclusive restorative impulse' (303) that repairs the organisation's emotional fabric and encourages a better and more trusting understanding of an emotional landscape (Gunter, Rogers, and Woods 2010) that reflects more acutely the experiences of work (Rothman 2008). The growth in re-spiritualising organisations (Casey 2002, 2004) and the rise of 'wellbeing' cultures (Warr 1978; Siontu 2005) ignites what Woods (2007) and Hartley (2010, 2019) depict as the affective and ethical rationality of the trusting organisation.

### The Mantelpiece

The Mantelpiece lens evidences practices that win the game, the *illusio,* and displays its silverware. Competition is reflected in mission statements, vision, and marketing strategies (Fitzgerald 2008). It is dependent upon cultures of continuous but inexpensive improvement, innovative yet replicable practice, and commonly agreed standards. Through performance management cultures and the embedding of formal hierarchical relationships between professionals, staff are presupposed to be docile and compliant, the result of which is a 'fragile, limited and tightly managed professionalism' (Hall 2013, 279) constricted by powerful external contexts. Compliant professionals are, according to Gold et al. (2003) positioned in the game as 'followers', inhabiting the periphery of the field but contributing to the powerful positions of those players centrally placed and in receipt or recognition of expert knowledges. Such players enjoy space to invent, and participate in the game as entrusted innovators of toolkits, consultations and best practice guides of 'what works'. In this way, central policy is 'evidenced', amplified by those followers on the edge of the action, and thus translated into local practice. Staff are empowered but into a potentially difficult environment (Fielding 1996) where ideas struggle against the performative restrictions of accountability, furthering the *illusio.*

### The Cuckoo

The Cuckoo lens focuses on unexpected disruptions, of contrast and resistance, of heterodox. It is a mutation whose presence interrupts the other metaphors and their recognisable surroundings. Mistaken by the other players, its strategy reveals the *illusio* of the game as the unchallenged acceptance of the rules in play, and the *doxa,* or misrecognised necessity for the game to be played. The Cuckoo lens disturbs fundamental and taken-for-granted assumptions by suggesting a potential anarchic reality and readjustment of power. Fielding (1996) suggests: 'Empowerment is thus not about giving power or allowing freedom of thought and action within a clearly defined sphere; it is about rupturing that sphere and shaping it anew' (406) and by reducing role boundaries and challenging hierarchies. The disruption of the Cuckoo creates an unsettling world view (King and Learmonth 2015) and its anarchic nature can affiliate with positions of resistance such as cynicism (Fleming and Spicer 2003) spirituality and sensual re-enchantments (Casey 2002) carnival (Fielding 2006) responsible dissent (Wright 2001) and the potential reconceptualisation of leading through humility and dialogue (Youngs 2008).

## The lens of powerful gameplay

I now turn to the contributions of the project participants as repositioned professionals, offering insight into the condition of the field. Through their utterance and observed practices, multiple but simultaneously held positions become apparent in what Bourdieu (1989) identifies as 'schemes of perception, thought and action' (14) within the organisation.

Bourdieu determines that the field is a competitive arena (Thomson 2008) and I suggest the Lock and Key and Mantelpiece lenses have strong dispositions towards playing a powerful game through their expertise in control and instrumentality.

Initially, the project considered the prevalence of hierarchical and performative responses in what Rayner and Gunter (2020) identify as the dynamic interplay between state positioning and professional position-taking. For example, Participant 8 explained Hillvale's approach and the implementation of mandated financial efficiencies:

> Staff are not always aware of the deliberately structured approach to the reforms that we have had to implement. The very first group of people that we looked at were SLT (senior leadership team) and then we looked at middle leaders and now it is hitting staff, so yes that was a deliberate attempt to try and take it from the top down and not the other way. (Participant 8)

Here the paternalistic power dynamic of the Lock and Key lens, that wishes to protect the resources of the organisation, is used by staff positioned with authority. However, although Participant 8 identifies how a top-down restructure of the college workforce was a response to the coalition government's policies (Belfield, Crawford, and Sibieta 2017), other participants experienced this process differently. No senior staff were displaced by reorganisation, although some members moved on, and an increased workload for the remaining membership ensued. However, other staff who had previously been structured lower down the hierarchy, found themselves removed and disorientated by their subsequent loss of capital. Participant 2 observes:

> There are a lot of people here who feel disengaged with their roles and feel decidedly down, (though) not downtrodden. I think there's a lot of people here who, through restructuring and other bits and pieces, feel not particularly positive towards the organization. (Participant 2)

Here an engagement group functions instrumentally to reinstate compliance (Fitzgerald 2008) amongst those displaced. The gatekeeping position of Hillvale's Lock and Key has little resistance to the reform agenda, and with it the growing utility of staff. Talk of the 'repetition of workload' (Participant 1) 'increased workload, increased class sizes' (Participant 13), and the 'constant treadmill' (Participant 5) where 'too much is happening all the time (Participant 7) is common. For the majority of staff, newly introduced job descriptions, timetable models and increased contact hours represent an erosion of professional resources exchanged, by the organisation, for efficiency savings and financial survival. The sense of impermanence and insecurity is heightened as the momentum of GERM deepens a sense of precarity. In his first interview, Participant 8 confesses: 'It's actually become increasingly difficult to do [everything] and with the best will in the world if there are little bits (of the job) that maybe … maybe that fall off. Hopefully nothing very important'. Similarly, Participant 1 reflects on the fragility of their position: 'I have lost my management time for my course, so I am on four free lessons per week. I know I get paid to manage a course but its nearly 200 students and it's out of control'.

Thus, capital is not exchanged, according to Bourdieu (1984), but lost to the decision-making elite and its absence causes disquiet that invented structures, like an engagement group, try to disarm. As the capital held by already powerful players structures the game's rules and logic as guiding principles (Gunter, Rogers, and Woods 2010), restricted and bound positions on the field strengthen the *doxa* of leadership as vital decision-making players. A traditional hierarchy where the college executive controls the discourse is described:

> Participant 12 on decision-making: 'generally I think that (SLT and Faculty Leaders) are quite centralized in bringing things together for decisions'. Participant 11 on consultation: 'It is important just to remind people that you are consulting them. It sounds stupid but sometimes we stand up and we tell them about things and I don't think people even register that that's consultation, but we have got much better at saying this is us consulting'. Participant 9 on staff voice: 'we aren't scared of staff views, certainly there was a phase of being very bothered'

## The lens of precarious gameplay

A context of continuous 'progress' requires that new policy directives are pushed through the system and so the high-risk demands of GERM justifies the need for 'leaders' and 'leading', and thus embedding the *illusio*. Although privileged within a hierarchical structure these positions are insecure. Participant 8 finds the pressure a challenge that is not unrewarding, but is increasingly stressful: 'it makes sure you are constantly reviewing everything you do and you try to do things better than you can, sometimes for less money. You have to be inventive don't you, and creative'. However, Participant 8 goes on to describe the limits of creativity when, following a slump in achievement data, an OFSTED inspection was triggered. The college's vulnerability was exposed once a disappointing overall effectiveness grade was published, and Hillvale endured the precarity of the marketplace:

> Hindsight is a wonderful thing isn't it because we had such a nice trajectory up to that point. There is something in saying that's the logical thing, to think it was ok; but we will never do that again. You have to interrogate everything really, really carefully and ultimately it's about ensuring that the students get the best possible outcomes that they can. (Participant 8)

The lenses of the Lock and Key and the Mantelpiece amplify the presence of, and justify the need for, powerful performative rule-makers at Hillvale. I observed surveillance and control mechanisms at the college operating through its various systems of performance monitoring, student reports, course assessments and recovery plans. These processes of individualisation (Bottery 2005) expose persons to scrutinised accountabilities and vulnerabilities through forensic investigations of their capabilities. Workers are reminded of why these surveillances are carried out when a short OFSTED inspection occurred during the project's timespan. Its report applauds the work of 'leaders', their use of performance management tools and their 'tireless' and 'relentless drive for continuous improvement', whist placing 'greater accountability' on teachers, 'improving teaching and learning', with 'actions for teachers' that 'help' and 'require' teachers 'to improve'; the *illusio* of performative accountability becomes deeply embedded.

Technical proficiency evidenced through data, standardised measurement and surveillance practices will inevitably, it seems, supersede professional knowledge and the performative *illusio* of the Mantelpiece sustains a *doxa* of GERM's elite hierarchy. Furthermore, the idealisation of the 'best teachers' and their 'best practice' both burdens the individual responsible for evidencing the accepted and celebrated view of professionalism espoused by senior staff, and disguises the continued proletarianisation (Ball 1987; Ozga and Lawn 1988) and de-professionalisation of the education service that, for Hartley (2019), combines 'digitally enhanced bureaucracy and market driven education policies' (11). Hence the Mantelpiece entrenches the *illusio* and Participant 2 offered this observation:

> I would suggest that in many organizations, especially in FE colleges, teachers have been turned into an artisan class, we are not professionals any more. They were turned into an artisan class about 10 years ago and that was through pay, that was through the way they were dealt with, that was through hourly paid staff. That was through, you know, being disempowered and having your rights taken off you, all sorts of ways. (Participant 2)

## The lens of therapeutic gameplay

As the Hillvale Project evolved, the purpose of an engagement group revealed further the contradictory positions on the field. As a product of Hillvale's culture, the engagement group could also re-culture the organisation and counteract the negative impacts of repositioning, through efforts described by Participant 13 as 'cushioning the blow'. Of the 20 events designed by the engagement group the majority offered a 'cohesive' response to the perceived structural fragmentation and disorientation noted by some Participants:

> 'There is an ambiguity in a way, because there are no such things as departments here, Ok? But then there are department-sort of rooms and offices, where people absolutely sort of stick to, cling to, from what I can see, and do not stray from' (Participant 2). 'The reality of that external accountability is filtering down and affecting everyone within the college.' (Participant 13) "What I really miss is that 'being with everybody'" (Participant 7), 'I thought we should just focus on ways of making staff feel happier at work, at reducing stress.' (Participant 3)

The Welcome Mat, as I came to understand it, initiated spaces where interpersonal actions are built through informal networks (Gunter, Rogers, and Woods 2010). Acting as an agent on the field the engagement group creates opportunities to structure an affective and therapeutic community that, through its practices, offers a deliberate counterpoint to comments like: 'I have no pals here, and so I never come here and enjoy, necessarily, the experiences of the day, and relationships, in all honesty' (Participant 2). Participant 7 develops this point succinctly:

> And I started to feel like I just come to work, do my work, don't speak to anyone, get your work done. You haven't got enough time, back out of here, then in again. Whereas there has (in) being part of the engagement group and bringing in things like staff rewards and seeing the lighter side, has completely reconnected me again now. (Participant 7)

More substantial engagement group events encouraged deliberate participation and interaction through explicit involvement whilst invigorating inter-connected relations. An event for a well-being day, now commonplace as a 'soft' leadership activity (Hartley 2019) across many organisations, illustrates this. Such an event is helpful in understanding how a response to professional repositioning may take shape. In this instance a physical and temporal space beyond the everyday running of the college had been set aside for a range of activities to happen, reflecting the engagement group's investment of its capital. The planned activities were not curriculum-focused or management-themed, and time was available on this day for all staff to be 'released' from professional duties.

Whilst participation in cross college networks nourishes the social fabric of the organisation, it is interesting to note that such activities are generally not integrated into the core actions of the organisation. A well-being day therefore, is distinct from meeting schedules, staff training, INSET and from 'learning community' groups typically 'officialised' into school and college best practices. Well-being days can represent a moment of unfettered freedom, when a group from outside the official hierarchy wins permission to take over the college and is reminiscent of the subversion of hierarchy through carnival (Fielding 2006). It offers a glimpse of the engagement group's potential, even though an embedded approach by the organisation to the impacts of GERM on professionals could generate a more sustained response. Participant 1 expresses these limitations: 'Well-being day? All happy on that day, but we won't be able to maintain the momentum'. Elsewhere events have been described as 'lipstick on a pig' and 'window dressing' (Participant 5), and Participants 2, 16 and 17 are all unsure of how or what an engagement group is capable of remedying.

## The lens of game-changing

Gunter (2016) states that position taking is a 'shared territory' (8) and the engagement group tried to enculture collegiality through a number of consultation exercises. Participant suggestions emerge that a group like this can model working relations and ways of interacting across the organisation that can alter professional practice:

> 'Staff (working) as a collective' (Participant 11), 'Knowing people on an individual level translates into better working relationships' (Participant 16), 'What can we do collectively rather than what can they do for me?' (Participant 12), and the engagement group is able to 'removes barriers' (Participant 9), or 'You will always have the staff on this side (gestures)and the SLT on this side (gestures), and thinking 'this about this' whereas are we not reconnecting everything? Because that's how I feel' (Participant 7), even: 'we represent so many different areas, we have got teaching staff, we've got managers, we've got support staff and premises (staff) so we've got a cross section ready' (Participant 3) and 'Sometimes it is not about curriculum stuff, it's about regular stuff, … We've got to involve everybody haven't we?' (Participant 17)

Similar dynamic potential is embraced by the executive. Descriptions like 'collective', 'democratic' 'voice', 'dialogue' and 'working together' punctuate the conversation. Participant 10 suggests the group is developmental in terms of personal goals and achievements, with members experiencing the role of leaders where previously it was difficult to get those voices heard: 'I see them being leaders now because they are leading on ideas'

(Participant 10). The engagement group is a useful structure in college, playing a vital role because it has 'done things' and is 'solutions based' (Participant 9), and it also 'tells us something about us' (Participant 10), the people of and within the organisation. The agentic potential of a group like this, perceived through the Cuckoo lens, emboldens professionals to think differently, question processes and be encouraged to 'speak back' and challenge the *illusio* that has maintained the *doxa* of the field by adopting a more powerful position.

However, fields are a struggle between established order and aspiring fractions (Bourdieu 1993). A vivid illustration occurred when the core values of the college culture were refocused as a tool and utility of behavioural management, and for which an external consultancy was contracted. I, as researcher, was perplexed but also intrigued by the underlying principles that rejected the practices and enculturing influence of an engagement group for this purpose. 'XYX' (a pseudonym) is a behaviour management consultancy, commissioned to work with Hillvale within the lifespan of the project.

XYX's own literature salutes the practices of official hierarchies: prescribing enactments of 'self-audits', adoption of 'reinforced routines', construction of 'tradition', and belief in 'exceptionally high standards' that 'inspires, motivates and creates profound cultural change' (unpaged). The literature contains an explicit homage to private education, where: 'the consistency of tradition is overwhelming, you cannot put a rizla paper between their consistent front' (unpaged). XYX is enraptured with concepts of elite and hierarchical structures that can regulate culture and the qualities of the Lock and Key are attributed to such a traditionalist approach. Its work also exemplifies the elaborate display that is embraced by the Mantelpiece at the heart of which reside performative acts of 'showing'. The 'XYX' approach is expressed through rituals and gestures that present visible confirmations of their transformational work. Pledges are made, ribbons are worn, mantras learnt, gestures practiced. I noted in my research dairy how the keynote speaker recounted, charismatically, the adventures that adopters of 'the system' have had, with a warning that those who do not like this game may no longer fit in and could be removed from the field, as in leave the organisation.

Such types of consultancy work in cultural formations is a technical asset, structuring the outputs and performances of staff and students. It is respected because it is perceived as benefitting the organisation's industrial production of good benchmark scores. It does not recognise a college as a cultural organisation responsible for cultural production, but as a high-performing and winning team. Therefore, dissenting voices are disapproved of and the power of the rational goal approach to cultural change takes seed. The adoption of XYX's agenda was not without contest from the staff, but Participants 12 and 13 as members of the executive, strongly defended XYX's transformational role. I suggest that XYX is incompatible with the design and purposes of an engagement group and can be recognised as a strong example of what makes such a group necessary. As an artefact of the field of power, XYX is an officially sanctioned violence, commissioned by the college's executive to force compliance to a narrow doctrine of performances.

However relevant its contribution, the executive limits the influence of groups like the engagement group. Bourdieu (1989) describes the constitution of such groups as a powerful leadership action 'by proxy', and of authorisation through 'a long process of institutionalization' (23). When these groups, as change agents, respond to shifting policy contexts, the dominant position of the executive is compromised. Accordingly,

98     EDUCATIONAL LEADERSHIP AND POLICY IN A TIME OF PRECARITY

despite investing its symbolic capital in the engagement group, the executive contracted consultants as preferred change agent, and the orthodoxy of the field remains unaltered.

## Re-focusing the lenses

If I attempt to refocus the lenses away from orthodoxy I have to be guided by Bourdieu and his formulations of a heterodox. The special quality of the Cuckoo is that, nested and undisclosed within the meanings of the other metaphors, it generates capital. And whilst its power as the heterodox is 'to reveal what is already there' (Bourdieu 1989, 23) its reflexivity, enabled here through the various acceptances that the engagement group experiences, is disguised by coherence, kinship and possession. The first hidden Cuckoo is an artefact of the cultural production of Hillvale's necessary and evident functional hierarchies, and, following Bourdieu's (1998) 'practical logic' (90), benefits from contradictory actions 'which reproduce in their own terms the logic from which coherence is generated' (92). Through the Lock and Key an engagement group is a manifestation of established coherence. Secondly, the hidden Cuckoo is an example of the conforming practices of kinship, accrued, according to Bourdieu (1990) through 'the symbolic profit secured by the approval, socially conferred, on practices conforming to the official representation of practices; that is the social kinship' (170). Practicable responses of the engagement group are officially sanctioned on the Welcome Mat, and relationships across the hierarchy are made tangible through practical and official enactments. These are moments of 'social kinship'. The third hidden Cuckoo conceives the engagement group as a gift, residing ornamentally on the Mantelpiece. According to Bourdieu (1990), the gift is an act of possession that binds the receiver into a debt of gratitude through which, in taking the gift, the recipient is taken possession of. If heterodoxy makes explicit the sum total of opposites (Bourdieu 1994) the project participants have, in various degrees as Cuckoo, become representatives of 'competing possibles' (165) through their association with the engagement group. Each Cuckoo contributes capital for the group and its members by exposing the reality of how that capital is constituted. Through reinvestment of its resources, the engagement group emerges from the Cuckoo lens as a fitting and potentially profound reply to the practices of professional repositioning. It exposes the *illusio* of performative practices of the field in order that the *doxa* of hierarchical power can be challenged through developing and strengthening the relationships knitting organisations together.

Whether this group, as an organisational and cultural response to the fluidity of professional positions, can address conflicting identities within the social universe (Bourdieu 1993) of Hillvale is an important question. But by recognising the 'special' part of the culture of Hillvale that produced the engagement group, the Cuckoo can be interpreted as something uncommon, or extraordinary. The Cuckoo, as a summation of all the metaphors, enables heterodoxy, and 'the recognition of multiple correct versions and possible constructions of reality' (Nolan 2012, 205) to nest in the college so that non-conformist attitudes and opinions find a space on the field of organisational power beyond the constraints of orthodoxy.

Metaphors that conceive organisations as communal, communitied, relational networks and person-centred (Greenfield 1993; Fielding 2001, 2006; Townsend 2013) must suffice personal and professional needs (Ball 1987), replenishing and nourishing the 'negotiated order of organizational life' (214) by constructing discursive forums for speaking out, or 'speaking back' (Fitzgerald 2008, 127). Heterodoxy, therefore, needs to escape the rationality of the grocer (Bourdieu 1998) and the endless stock-taking and accounting that obfuscates the true purpose of education, by appreciating the moral tones of responsibility and reciprocity. A Cuckoo 'space' where 'people can come together and reflect, as equals, on matters of mutual importance' (Fielding 2009, 449), could encourage professionals to think philosophically about what they are doing and why (Ball 2016). Neither resource, utility, nor separation between staff and leaders, but a combination of all, a Cuckoo is where people resolve the conflicts of the values that augment their critical consciousness. I suggest, above all, this 'space' should exist within the organisation's imagination, free to make sense of constituent communities, interpreting and understanding their significance and purpose in and with the organisation. In so doing I claim that a response to professional repositioning can be one that speaks back to the global crisis endured by education professionals with confidence.

## Summary

I have suggested here that groups such as an engagement group can provide a resistance to the domination of symbolic violence (Schubert 2008) that is represented by GERM through curriculum design, the competitive eagerness to demonstrate success, and the routines of failing that are internalised by staff and students as their 'individual problem' (Apple 1985, 59). As Bourdieu (1989) indicates, making visible and explicit what is hidden and implicit, or that which made necessary the existence of the group to begin with, is 'power par excellence' (23). In reconstructing the world of domination, as making a space for heterodoxy does, an invitation for alternative theories of further education is made. To lift this, or some similar group, into an activist (Apple 2013) rather than a utilitarian role, is a challenging practice for professionals and academics alike, yet assimilating the anarchist traits of the Cuckoo as a practical response to a redistribution of organisational power is surely a suitable response to the orthodoxy of education reforms.

## Acknowledgements

I would like to thank Steven J. Courtney for his guidance and support in the production of this article through its various drafts, and to the referees for their constructive and helpful comments.

## Disclosure statement

No potential conflict of interest was reported by the author(s).

## References

Alvesson, M., and A. Spicer. 2016. "(Un)Conditional Surrender? Why Do Professionals Willingly Comply with Managerialism." *Journal of Organizational Change Management* 29 (1): 29–45.

Apple, M. J. 1985. *Education and Power*. Boston: Ark.

Apple, M. J. 2008. "Can Schooling Contribute to a More Just Society?" *Education, Citizenship and Social Justice* 3 (1): 239–261.

Apple, M. J. 2011. "Democratic Education in Neoliberal and Neoconservative Times." *International Studies in Sociology of Education* 21 (1): 21–31.

Apple, M. J. 2013. *Can Education Change Society*. London: Routledge.

Ball, S. J. 1987. *The Micro-Politics of the School: Towards a Theory of School Organization*. London: Routledge.

Ball, S. J. 1993. "Education Markets, Choice and Social Class: The Market as a Class Strategy in the UK and the USA." *British Journal of Sociology of Education* 14 (1): 3–19.

Ball, S. J. 2006. *Education, Policy and Social Class, The Selected Works of Stephen J. Ball*. London: Routledge.

Ball, S. J. 2008. *The Education Debate*. Bristol: Policy Press.

Ball, S. J. 2016. "Neoliberal Education? Confronting the Slouching Beast." *Policy Futures in Education* 14 (8): 1046–1059.

Barker, B. 2008. "School Reform Policy in England Since 1988: Relentless Pursuit of the Unattainable." *Journal of Education Policy* 23 (6): 669–683.

Belfield, C., C. Crawford, and L. Sibieta. 2017. *Long-run Comparisons of Spending per Pupil Across Different Stages of Education*. London: Institute for Fiscal Studies.

Bottero, W. 2009. "Relationality and Social Interaction." *The British Journal of Sociology* 60 (2): 399–420.

Bottery, M. 2000. *Education, Policy and Ethics*. London: Continuum.

Bottery, M. 2005. "The Individualization of Consumption A Trojan Horse in the Destruction of the Public Sector." *Education Management Administration and Leadership* 33 (3): 267–288.

Boulton, D., and M. Hammersley. 2006. "Analysis of Unstructured Data." In *Data Collection and Analysis*, Second Ed., edited by R. Sapford and V. Jupp, 243–259. London: Sage.

Bourdieu, P. 1984. *Distinction*. London: Routledge.

Bourdieu, P. 1989. "Social Space and Symbolic Power." *Sociological Theory* 7 (1): 14–25.

Bourdieu, P. 1990. *The Logic of Practice*. Cambridge: Polity Press.

Bourdieu, P. 1993. *The Field of Cultural Production*. Cambridge: Polity Press.

Bourdieu, P. 1994. "Structure, Habitus Power, a Basis for a Theory of Symbolic Power." In *Culture Power History: a Reader in Contemporary Social Theory*, edited by N. B. Dirks, G. Eley, and S. B. Ortner, 155–199. Chichester: Princetown University Press.

Bourdieu, P. 1998. *Acts of Resistance*. Cambridge: Polity Press.

Boxenbaum, E., and L. Rouleau. 2011. "New Knowledge Products as Bricolage: Metaphors as Scripts in Organizational Theory." *Academy of Management Review* 36 (2): 272–296.

Briggs, A. R. J. 2004. "Finding the Niche? Competition and Collaboration for Sixth Form College." *Education + Training* 46 (3): 119–126.

Butler, J. 2016. *Frames of War: When is Life Grievable?* London: Verso.

Casey, C. 2002. *Critical Analysis of Organisations: Theory, Practice, Revitalization*. London: Sage.

Casey, C. 2003. "The Learning Worker, Organizations and Democracy." *International Journal of Lifelong Education* 22 (6): 620–634.

Casey, C. 2004. "Bureaucracy Re-Enchanted? Spirit, Experts and Authority in Organization." *Organization* 11 (1): 59–79.

Ceulemans, C., S. Maarten, and E. Struyf. 2012. "Professional Standards for Teachers: how do They 'Work'? An Experiment in Tracing Standardisation in-the-Making in Teacher Education." *Pedagogy Culture and Society* 20 (1): 29–47.

Choudry, S., and J. Williams. 2017. "Figured Worlds in the Field of Power." *Mind, Culture, and Activity* 24 (3): 247–257.

Cornellissen, J. P. 2005. "beyond Compare: Metaphor in the Organization Theory." *Academy of Management Review* 30 (4): 751–764.

Courtney, S. J. 2015. "Corporatized Leadership in English Schools." *Journal of Educational Administration and History* 47 (3): 214–231.

Courtney, S. J., and H. M. Gunter. 2015. "Get Off My Bus! School Leaders, Vision Work and the Elimination of Teachers." *International Journal of Leadership in Education* 18 (4): 395–417.

Courtney, S. J., and R. McGinity. 2020. "System Leadership as Depoliticisation: Reconceptualising Educational Leadership in a New Multi-Academy Trust." *Educational Management Administration and Leadership* 20 (10): 1–18.

Dow, A., R. Hattam, A. Reid, G. Shacklock, and J. Smyth. 2000. *Teachers' Work in a Globalizing Economy.* London: Routledge.

Eacott, S. 2013. "Towards a Theory of School Leadership Practice: A Bourdieusian Perspective." *Journal of Educational Administration and History* 45 (2): 174–188.

Ferrare, J. J., and M. W. Apple. 2015. "Field Theory and Educational Practice: Bourdieu and the Pedagogic Qualities of Local Field Positions in Educational Contexts." *Cambridge Journal of Education* 45 (1): 43–59.

Fielding, M. 1996. "Empowerment: Emancipation or Enervation?" *Journal of Education Policy* 11 (3): 399–417.

Fielding, M. 2001. "Ofsted, Inspection and the Betrayal of Democracy." *Journal of Philosophy of Education* 35 (4): 695–701.

Fielding, M. 2006. "Leadership, Radical Student Engagement and the Necessity of Person-Centred Education." *International Journal of Leadership in Education* 9 (4): 299–313.

Fielding, M. 2009. "Public Space and Educational Leadership: Reclaiming and Renewing Our Radical Traditions." *Educational Management Administration & Leadership* 37 (4): 497–521.

Fitzgerald, T. 2008. "The Continuing Politics of Mistrust: Performance Management and the Erosion of Professional Work." *Journal of Educational Administration and History* 40 (2): 113–128.

Fleming, P., and A. Spicer. 2003. "Working at a Cynical Distance: Implications for Power, Subjectivity and Resistance." *Organization* 10 (1): 157–179.

Flusberg, S. J., T. Teenie Matlock, and P. H. Thibodeau. 2018. "War Metaphors in Public Discourse." *Metaphor and Symbol* 33 (1): 1–18.

Foster, W. 2004. "The Decline of the Local: A Challenge to Educational Leadership." *Educational Administration Quarterly* 40 (2): 176–191.

Fuller, K., and H. Stevenson. 2019. "Global Education Reform: Understanding the Movement." *Educational Review* 71 (1): 1–4.

Gardner, P. 2019. "The GERM is Spreading: A Report from Australia." *Literacy Today* 91: 8–11.

Gergen, K. J. 2003. "Action Research and Orders of Democracy." *Action Research* 1 (1): 39–56.

Gewirtz, S., and S. J. Ball. 2000. "From 'Welfarism' to 'New Managerialism': Shifting Discourses of School Headship in the Education Marketplace." *Discourse: Studies in the Cultural Politics of Education* 21 (3): 253–268.

Gibson, W., and A. Brown. 2009. *Working with Qualitative Data.* London: Sage.

Gold, A., J. Evans, P. Earley, D. Halpin, and P. Collarbone. 2003. "Principled Principals? Values-Driven Leadership: Evidence from Ten Case Studies of 'Outstanding' School Leaders." *Educational Management & Administration* 31 (2): 127–138.

Gray, A., and B. Jenkins. 1993. "Codes of Accountability in the New Public Sector." *Accounting, Auditing & Accountability Journal* 6 (3): 52–67.

Greany, T., and R. Higham. 2018. *Hierarchy Markets and Networks: Analysing the 'Self-Improving School-led System' Agenda in England and the Implications for Schools.* London: Institute of Education Press.

Greenfield, T. 1993. *Greenfield on Educational Administration.* Edited by T. Greenfield and P. Ribbins. London: Routledge.

Gulson, K. N., S. Lewis, B. Lingard, C. Lubienski, K. Takayama, and P. T. Webb. 2017. "Policy Mobilities and Methodology: A Proposition for Inventive Methods in Education Policy Studies." *Critical Studies in Education* 58 (2): 224–241.

Gunter, H. M. 2016. *An Intellectual History of School; Leadership, Practice and Research*. London: Bloomsbury Academic.

Gunter, H. M., and D. Hall. 2013. "Trust in Education, Teachers and Their Work." In *Trust and Confidence in Government and Public Services*, edited by S. Llewellyn, S. Brooks, and A. Mahon, 204–220. London: Routledge.

Gunter, H. M., S. Rogers, and C. Woods. 2010. "Personalization, the Individual, Trust and Education in a Neo-Liberal World." In *Trust and the Betrayal in Educational Administration and Leadership*, edited by E. A. Samier and M. Schmidt, 119–215. London: Routledge.

Hall, D. 2013. "Drawing a Veil Over Managerialism: Leadership and the Discursive Disguise of the New Public Management." *Journal of Educational Administration and History* 45 (3): 267–228.

Hall, D., H. Gunter, and J. Bragg. 2012. "Leadership, New Public Management and the re-Modelling and Regulation of Teacher Identities." *International Journal of Leadership in Education: Theory and Practice* 16 (2): 173–190.

Hall, D., and R. McGinity. 2015. "Conceptualizing Teacher Professional Identity in Neoliberal Times: Resistance, Compliance and Reform." *Education Policy Analysis Archives* 23 (88): 1–21.

Hardy, J. 2015. "The Institutional, Structural and Agential Embeddedness of Precarity." *Warsaw Forum of Economic Sociology* 6 (11): 1–19.

Hartley, D. 1997. "The New Managerialism in Education: a Mission Impossible?" *Cambridge Journal of Education* 27 (1): 47–57.

Hartley, D. 2010. "The Management of Education and the Social Theory of the Firm: From Distributed Leadership to Collaborative Community." *Journal of Educational Administration and History* 42 (4): 345–361.

Hartley, D. 2019. "The Emergence of Blissful Thinking in the Management of Education." *British Journal of Educational Studies* 67 (2): 201–216.

Heffernan, A. 2019. "The 'Punk Rock Principal': A Metaphor for Rethinking Educational Leadership." *Journal of Educational Administration and History* 51 (2): 117–133.

Heffernan, A., D. Netolicky, and N. Mockler. 2019. "Special Issue Using Metaphors to Explore School Leadership: Possibilities, Problems and Pitfalls." *Journal of Educational Administration and History* 51: 2.

Hodkinson, P., and M. Bloomer. 2000. "Stokingham Sixth Form College: Institutional Culture and Dispositions to Learning." *British Journal of Sociology of Education* 21 (2): 187–202.

Hughes, B., H. Gunter, and S. Courtney. 2019. "Researching Professional Biographies of Educational Professionals in new Dark Times." *British Journal of Educational Studies* 68 (3): 275–293.

King, D., and M. Learmonth. 2015. "Can Critical Management Studies Ever be 'Practical'? A Case Study in Engaged Scholarship." *Human Relations* 68 (3): 353–375.

Lakoff, G., and M. Johnson. 2003. *Metaphors We Live By*. Chicago, IL: University of Chicago Press.

Lazar, S., and A. Sanchez. 2019. "Understanding Labour Politics in an Age of Precarity." *Dialectical Anthropology* 43 (3): 2–14.

Lingard, B., S. Sellar, A. Hogan, and G. Thompson. 2017. *Commercialisation in Public Schooling (CIPS)*. Sydney, NSW: News South Wales Teachers Federation.

Lumby, J. 2003a. *Accountability in Further Education: The Impact of UK Government Policy*, paper presented to AERA annual meeting, April 2003. Accessed, 26/10/2014. www.academia.edu/26916080/Accountability_in_Further_Education_The_Impact_of_UK_Government_Policy.

Lumby, J. 2003b. "Culture Change: The Case of Sixth Form and General Further Education Colleges Educational." *Management Administration & Leadership* 31 (2): 159–174.

Maguire, M., and A. Braun. 2019. "Headship as Policy Narration: Generating Metaphors of Leading in the English Primary School." *Journal of Educational Administration and History* 51 (2): 103–116.

Mavers, D., B. Somekh, and J. Restorick. 2002. "Interpreting the Externalised Images of Pupils' Conceptions of ICT: Methods for the Analysis of Concept Maps." *Computers & Education* 38: 187–207.

McGinity, R. 2015. "Innovation and Autonomy at a Time of Rapid Reform: An English Case Study." *Nordic Journal of Studies in Educational Policy* 1: 62–72.

Merkens, H. 2004. "Selection Procedures Sampling and Case Construction." In *A Companion to Qualitative Research, Translated by B Jenner*, edited by U. Flick, E. Von Kardoff, and I. Steinke, 165–171. London: Sage.

Netolicky, D. M. 2019. "redefining Leadership in Schools: The Cheshire Cat as Unconventional Metaphor." *Journal of Educational Administration and History* 51 (2): 149–164.

Newman, J. 2004. "Constructing Accountability: Network Governance and Managerial Agency." *Public Policy and Administration* 19 (4): 17–24.

Newman, J. 2005. "Bending Bureaucracy: Leadership and Multi-Level Governance." In *The Values of Bureaucracy*, edited by P. du Gay, 191–209. Oxford: Oxford University Press.

Nolan, K. 2012. "Dispositions in the Field: Viewing Mathematics Teacher Education Through the Lens of Bourdieu's Social Field Theory." *Educational Studies in Mathematics* 80: 201–215.

Ortenblad, A., L. Putnam, and K. Trehan. 2016. "Beyond Morgan's Eight Metaphors: Adding to and Developing Organization Theory." *Human Relations* 69 (4): 875–889.

Ozga, O., and M. Lawn. 1988. "Schoolwork: Interpreting the Labour Process of Teaching." *British Journal of Sociology of Education* 9 (3): 323–336.

Page, D. 2017. "Conspicuous Practice: Self-Surveillance and Commodification in Education." *International Studies in Sociology of Education* 27 (4): 375–390.

Peters, M. A. 2017. "From State Responsibility for Education and Welfare to Self-Responsibilization in the Market." *Discourse: Studies in the Cultural Politics of Education* 38 (1): 138–145.

Pollitt, C. 2014. Management Redux? Keynote Address to the 2014 EIASM Conference, Edinburgh. Accessed 11/9/2018. https://soc.kuleuven.be/io/nieuws/managerialism-redux.pdf.

Rayner, S. M., and H. M. Gunter. 2020. "Resistance, Professional Agency and the Reform of Education in England." *London Review of Education* 18 (2): 265–280.

Ricoeur, P. 1978. "The Metaphorical Process as Cognition, Imagination, and Feeling." *Critical Inquiry, (Special Issue on Metaphor)* 5 (1): 143–159.

Riddle, S., and M. W. Apple. 2019. "Education and Democracy in Dangerous Times." In *Re-imagining Education for Democracy*, edited by S. Riddle and M. W. Apple, 1–11. London: Routledge.

Robinson, J., and C. Burke. 1996. "Tradition Culture and Ethos: The Impact of the Further and Higher Education Act (1992) on Sixth Form Colleges and Their Futures." *Evaluation and Research in Education* 10 (1): 3–22.

Rothman, S. 2008. "Job Satisfaction, Occupational Stress, Burnout and Work Engagement as Components of Work -Related Wellbeing." *South African Journal of Industrial Psychology* 34 (3): 11–16.

Samier, E. A. 2019. "The Theory and Uses of Metaphor in Educational Administration and Leadership: A Rejoinder." *Journal of Educational Administration and History* 51 (2): 182–195.

Schechter, C., H. Shaked, S. Ganon-Shilon, and M. Goldratt. 2018. "Leadership Metaphors: School Principals' Sense-Making of a National Reform." *Leadership and Policy in Schools* 17 (1): 1–26.

Schon, D. A. 1993. "Generative Metaphor: A Perspective on Problem-Setting in Social Policy." In *Metaphor and Thought, Second Edition*, edited by A. Ortony, 254–283. Cambridge: Cambridge University Press.

Schubert, J. D. 2008. "Suffering/ Symbolic Violence." In *Pierre Bourdieu, Key Concepts*, edited by M. Grenfell, 183–198. Durham: Acumen.

Shorter, P. 1994. "Sixth-Form Colleges and Incorporation: Some Evidence from Case Studies in the North of England." *Oxford Review of Education* 20 (4): 461–473.

Siontu, E. 2005. "The Rise of an Ideal: Tracing Changing Discourses of Wellbeing." *The Sociological Review* 53 (2): 255–275.

Sixth Form Colleges Association. 2020. Key Facts and Figures. https://sfcawebsite.s3.amazonaws.com/uploads/document/24711-SFCA-Key-Facts-2020-AW-Interactive2.pdf?t=1593419685.

Skerritt, C. 2019. "Discourse and Teacher Identity in Business-Like Education." *Policy Futures in Education* 17 (2): 153–171.

Smyth, J. 2011. "The Disaster of the 'Self-Managing School' – Genesis, Trajectory, Undisclosed Agenda, and Effects." *Journal of Educational Administration and History* 43 (2): 95–117.

Standing, G. 2011. *The Precariat, the New Dangerous Class*. London: Bloomsbury.

Stoten, D. W. 2014. "Authentic Leadership in English Education: What do College Teachers Tell us?" *International Journal of Educational Management* 28 (5): 510–522.

Thomson, P. 2008. "Field." In *Pierre Bourdieu, Key Concepts*, edited by M. Grenfell, 67–81. Durham: Acumen.

Thomson, P. 2017. *Educational Leadership and Pierre Bourdieu (Critical Studies in Educational Leadership, Management and Administration)*. London: Routledge.

Townsend, A. 2013. "Principled Challenges for a Participatory Discipline." *Educational Action Research* 21 (3): 326–342.

Warr, P. 1978. "A Study of Psychological Well-Being." *British Journal of Psychology* 69: 111–121.

Weick, K. E. 1989. "Theory Construction as Disciplined Imagination." *Academy of Management Review* 14 (4): 516–531.

Woods, P. 2007. "Within You and Without You: Leading Towards Democratic Communities." *Management in Education* 21 (4): 38–43.

Wright, N. 2001. "Leadership, Bastard Leadership and Managerialism, Confronting Twin Paradoxes of the Blair Education Project." *Education Management and Administration* 29 (3): 275–290.

Yin, R. K. 2016. *Qualitative Research from Start to Finish*. New York: Guildford Press.

Youngs, H. 2008, April 30 – May 3. "Should I Stand Back, or Should I Lead? Developing Intentional Communal Cultures of Emergent and Distributed Forms of Leadership in Educational Settings." Enhancing the Heart, Enriching the Mind, NZEALS International Educational Leadership Conference, Auckland.

# Necessary risk: addressing precarity by re-envisioning teaching and learning

Jeanne M. Powers ⓘ and Lok-Sze Wong ⓘ

**ABSTRACT**

In Arizona, the expansion and elaboration of neoliberal educational policies over the past three decades in Arizona have placed public schools and the teaching profession in precarious positions. These challenges have been compounded by the COVID-19 pandemic. Within this turbulent context, a school district in partnership with a college of education created and implemented a demonstration school aimed at re-envisioning how students learn and how teachers work. We analyse how district leaders responded to competing interests and pressures from the political environment and constituents as they designed, implemented, and expand this reform. We conclude by assessing how the features of the demonstration school, Arizona's public schooling environment, and the uncertainties introduced by the pandemic provide affordances and challenges for the reform's likelihood of survival.

## Introduction

In Arizona, the state legislature's efforts to expand and elaborate neoliberal educational policies over the past three decades – defunding, deregulation, marketisation, and privatisation – have created a precarious environment for public education as an institution and teaching as a profession.[1] These challenges have been compounded by the far-reaching effects of the COVID-19 pandemic in social, political, and economic life. Within this turbulent context, a public school district in partnership with a college of education created Aprender, a demonstration school aimed at re-envisioning how students learn and how teachers work.[2]

We document how as they designed, implemented, and expand this reform, public school district leaders (hereafter district leaders) often have to balance politically oppositional pressures and demands on public education. Our focus is on 'what precarity does' (Millar 2017, 5) at the institutional level by providing an analysis of a 'little-p' policy that is being enacted by school leaders in a local setting to respond to state policies associated with neoliberalism (Ball 2013, 8). Our analysis has implications for understanding how school leaders in other contexts might navigate the challenges posed by such policies. We also address how historically, similar reforms foundered in less challenging environments (Cuban 1993).

## Arizona's precarious public schooling environment

The US educational system is highly decentralised. Authority for public education is delegated to US states as a 'reserved' power under the Tenth Amendment to the US Constitution (Corcoran and Goertz 2005, 31). US state legislatures, in turn, delegate most decisions about instruction and the operation of public schools to local school districts. Similarly, most funding for US public schools comes from state or local governments; the latter are primarily from property taxes. In 2016–17, 12% of public school funding in Arizona was provided by the federal government, 47% came from the state, and the remaining 41% came from local sources (Hussar et al. 2020). Since 1997, Arizona has consistently ranked in the bottom five US states in per pupil funding from these sources (National Science Board 2020). In the wake of the Great Recession of 2008, the Arizona legislature cut its already low state funding for public schools while enacting corporate and income tax cuts.[3]

While a statewide teachers strike in 2018 forced the state legislature to re-invest in public education after a long period of disinvestment, Arizona continues to fund public schools below pre-recession levels (Leachman 2019). This long-term underfunding of public education is likely one factor driving a severe teacher shortage in the state. In December 2019, a survey of 209 school resource personnel indicated that Arizona schools had 7500 vacant teaching positions. Just over half were filled by individuals who did not meet standard teaching requirements, such as teachers who were pending certification or emergency-certified (Arizona School Personnel Administrators Association 2019). Approximately one quarter were filled by hiring long term substitute teachers, increasing class sizes, or reducing teachers' planning time.

The Arizona legislature has also been also aggressively privatising public education for more than two decades through a series of neoliberal education policies that deregulated and commodified public schooling and expanded the use of public funds to support private schools (Ball 2013; Standing 2014; Whitty 1997). In 1994 the Arizona legislature passed legislation authorising charter schools. Charter schools are public schools of choice governed by private entities rather than school districts. They are also exempt from some state regulations that school districts must comply with (Powers 2009). Arizona is among the five US states with the fewest restrictions on charter school operations (Center for Education Reform 2021). For example, Arizona's charter school law allows for-profit charter school management organisations to operate charter schools. There are well-documented instances of charter school operators profiting from their school's business arrangements, including a state legislator who made $13.9 million by selling the charter schools he owned and operated to a non-profit company (Harris 2018).

The 1994 legislation authorising charter schools included a provision for interdistrict choice, another form of marketisation. Interdistrict choice policies allow students to enrol in any public school in and outside their school districts of residence other than their assigned public school. Because state funding is tied to student enrolment, charter schools and interdistrict choice have created a competitive market for public school students in Arizona whereby both school districts and charter schools engage in marketing and create specialised programmes to attract students (Bernstein et al. 2021; Potterton 2019; see also Ball 2013 more generally).

Alongside these policies that expanded the marketisation and deregulation of public education, the Arizona legislature is also deeply committed to privatising education via mechanisms that channel state funding to private schools. In 1998 the legislature established the first of a set of tax credits that allow families to offset the cost of tuition at private schools. In 2019, individual taxpayers claimed just under $111 million in private school tax credits; a similar corporate tax credit channelled another $94 million that would have been collected as general revenue to private schools (Arizona Department of Revenue 2020). In 2011, Arizona was the first state to enact a programme that provides 'Empowerment Scholarship Accounts' (ESA) to parents of specific groups of students who opt out of the public school system. Parents approved for an ESA receive a debit card funded with 90% of the state dollars that would have been allocated to the district or charter school they left; they can use these funds to pay for the alternative educational services they choose for their children. Despite a 2018 voter referendum limiting the scope of the programme, the Republican-dominated state legislature continues to expand the ESA programme.

Finally, the COVID-19 pandemic has far-reaching implications for public schools that are still unfolding. All public schools in the state were closed for in-person instruction for the last quarter of the 2019–20 school year. In the fall of 2020, most school districts started the school year with remote learning. Because Arizona was one of the US states with the highest COVID-19 infection rates for most of 2020, many districts continued offering instruction remotely until March 2021 when the Governor issued an executive order that required all schools to open for in-person instruction. During this period, teachers' concerns about health and safety touched off a wave of retirements and resignations in Arizona that outpaced those in other states (Arizona School Personnel Administrators Association 2020; Bauerlein and Koh 2020; Will, Gewertz, and Schwartz 2020). School districts also face the increased costs of managing health and safety during the pandemic during a period when state budgets and the prospects for economic recovery are uncertain (Center on Budget and Policy Priorities 2020).

Thus, in Arizona, neoliberal education policies have created a particularly precarious institutional environment for public schools and, in the case described here, created incentives for district leaders to take risks aimed at attenuating some of the effects of these policies for the public schools they administer and expanding learning opportunities for students. In 2017, District leaders in the Desert Star School District, in partnership with Western University College of Education (WUCOE),[4] embarked on an ambitious project aimed at re-envisioning how teachers teach and how students learn. Desert Star leaders and their WUCOE partners designed and implemented Aprender, a demonstration school that combines: (a) teachers working in distributed-expertise teams of three or more, (b) a student-centered curriculum that fosters deeper and personalised learning, and (c) a reconfigured physical space to support the model.

The ways Desert Star leaders and their WUCOE partners responded to competing interests and pressures from constituents and the broader political environment presents both affordances and challenges for the reform's likelihood of survival. Our analysis draws upon data we jointly collected to analyse the design, implementation, and expansion of the demonstration school and includes: observations of meetings related to the implementation and expansion of the model school beginning six months before its launch, documents collected over a three-year period, interviews with key Desert Star district leaders and WUCOE partners, parent and student surveys conducted in May 2020, parent focus groups conducted in October 2020, weekly observations conducted at Aprender before schools in Arizona closed for in-person learning because of the COVID-19 pandemic, and regular observations while students learned remotely during the 2020–21 school year.[5]

## Conceptual framework

Our conceptual framework adapts Carnoy and Levin's (1985) argument that education is both a state function serving the needs of an advanced capitalist society and a site for social negotiation and conflict.[6] In this view, schools both reproduce and can be a site for contesting or ameliorating social inequality. Schools prepare students for the demands of the contemporary post-industrial capitalist workplace which privileges knowledge production and sorts them into differentiated roles within that system of economic organisation (Bowles and Gintis 1976; Labaree 1997; Peters 2012). At the same time, social movements and reformers have contested and blunted these reproductive functions by demanding through civic and court action that schools serve all students more equitably. Because it made equality a 'central commitment of [US] schools' (Minow 2010, 5), *Brown v. Board of Education* (1954) was a key turning point for the latter because it gave reformers outside of schools a foothold in their advocacy for equity-oriented policies beyond equality of access. Yet another cross-current is the expansion of school choice policies that have eroded the commitment to education as a public good (Labaree 1997). Carnoy and Levin (1985) argue that educators have to negotiate the competing concerns and interests of the business community that schools produce workers, demands for equity and calls for school choice from the public, and the internal concerns and interests of teachers and other members of the education bureaucracy as a professional group within an increasingly marketised system of public education.

Carnoy and Levin (1985) also provide a useful framework for analysing how the reforms proposed or enacted by educators, policymakers, and other reformers address perceived or explicit pressures from these constituents. Microtechnical reforms are small-scale reforms that do not require major organisational change, such as adding new subjects to the curriculum or the adoption of technology. Macrotechnical reforms are larger-scale reforms aimed at changing how schools are organised and what is taught, and include team teaching, open classrooms, and mastery learning. Micropolitical reforms are changes in internal decision making structures within schools (e.g. decentralised decision making) and the organisation of instruction (e.g. student participation in instructional decisions), while macropolitical reforms are systems-level changes in the governance of schools. The latter encompass neoliberal reforms aimed at deregulating, marketising, and privatising schools and democratic decentralisation such as community controlled schools. Aprender, the demonstration school we describe combines a unique set of macrotechnical, micropolitical, and macropolitical reforms aimed at: preparing students for the workplace under advanced capitalism, responding to the marketisation of public education, and promoting equitable access to educational opportunities.

## Aprender, a demonstration school

Desert Star leaders worked in close collaboration with WUCOE partners to design Aprender, a demonstration school aimed at (a) engaging students in a dynamic, student-centered learning environment, (b) creating new teacher roles and staffing structures to support student learning and reinvigorate the teaching profession, and (c) providing an open, flexible-use physical space that supports these reconfigured learning and teaching arrangements. Desert Star is a medium-sized suburban school district in the Southwest. In 2017–18, when Aprender was launched, approximately 40% of the district's students qualified for free and reduced lunch, the median among the surrounding and adjacent districts and 10% lower than the state average. The district serves a multiracial population of students: 44% of the district's students were identified as white, 29% as Latinx, 10% as Black, 6% as Asian American, 4% as American Indian, and the remaining 7% as multi-racial.[7] Over two-and-a half years, Desert Star district leaders and its WUCOE partner designed Aprender. They identified five design principles for the demonstration school: (a) student-centered learning experiences; (b) educators as designers and facilitators; (c) culture of community, care, and collaboration; (d) equity and inclusion; and (e) transformative learning spaces.

## Bridging multiple pressures

Aprender reflects the tensions of public schooling described by Carnoy and Levin (1985) whereby the demands of the workplace in an advanced capitalist society and demands for equity have to be balanced within the context of a highly marketised environment. In the following sections, we detail how Desert Star leaders and their WUCOE partners wove together a set of macrotechnical, micropolitical, and macropolitical reforms with the goal of creating an innovative school while also responding to the pressures on Arizona's public schools we detailed in the introduction.

### *Progressive curriculum and pedagogies*

The teaching and learning at Aprender are a macrotechnical reform in that the teachers are enacting a student-centered, project-based, and multi-disciplinary curriculum and pedagogies in mixed-age classrooms (Berger, Woodfin, and Vilen 2016).[8] In many ways, Aprender's pedagogical approach is aligned with John Dewey's vision for schools that provide child-centred, active learning experiences organised around cross-curricular problems or driving questions (Dewey 2017; see also Semel 1999). As such, it differs from how teaching and learning is organised in most US classrooms: teacher-centered, direct-instruction on content delivered in age-based grades that centres knowledge and skills from single subjects. This macrotechnical reform addresses pressures from education reformers and families for learning opportunities that engage children in deep and experiential learning around real-world problems.

The curriculum and pedagogies are also a micropolitical reform because Aprender students have opportunities to decide what they learn, how they learn it, and how they demonstrate their learning. Within the classroom, the teachers developed policies and practices aimed at scaffolding and supporting students' development as self-directed learners. Students also engage in 'passion projects' that provide structured opportunities for them to engage in inquiries about topics of their choice.

To some extent, the macrotechnical and micropolitical features of the curriculum and pedagogies were intended to address the widely-shared concern that schools are not effectively preparing students for jobs of the future (e.g. Lake 2019). For example, as Aprender was rolled out, district leaders emphasised that members of the business community were highly supportive of the demonstration school's pedagogical approach because they viewed it as a way to train future workers to creatively address complex problems. At public presentations, district staff used a short video to explain why they created Aprender. The video was narrated by a young woman off screen. A series of images flashed to illustrate two claims: (a) while our technologies have changed since 1900, schools have not; and (b) schools need to prepare students for the knowledge economy.

Because it evokes the vision of teaching and learning that John Dewey and other pedagogical progressives proposed over a century ago, the model of teaching and learning enacted at Aprender is not new (Reese 2005; see also Dewey 1938, 2017). While Dewey's critique of traditional teacher-centered education is well-known, he was also a critic of extreme forms of child-centred education. As Reese (2005) observed '[Dewey] sought a clear path apart from traditionalists who wanted a textbook-dominated classroom filled with passive students and romantics who glorified the child's freedom unchecked by teacher guidance and authority' (140; see also Labaree 2010). Although Dewey's *ideas* were influential, the *practices* associated with his ideas were never widely implemented (Labaree 2010; Mehta 2013). We return to this point when we discuss the prospects for Aprender.

### A team of educators

Aprender's staffing model combines macrotechnical and micropolitical reforms. As a macrotechnical reform, district leaders and WUCOE partners re-envisioned staffing around a six-teacher team supporting 120 students. As one district leader explained, 'It's how do you maximize your student-to-adult ratio in a way that isn't the standard one teacher per every 30 children.' Desert Star leaders intended this ratio to be cost-neutral: the salary for six adults in a team that includes student teachers is approximately the same as four teachers working independently in traditional classrooms. In its first year, the educator team consisted of a lead teacher, two experienced teachers, three full-time student teachers, and expert volunteers brought in on an ad hoc basis. Two members of the team had specialised training in special education and gifted education, respectively.

As a micropolitical reform, the team shares the roster of students and leverage their different areas of expertise and interest to collaboratively design student-centered learning experiences. The team has more authority over instructional decision-making than teachers in most schools (García 2020). For instance, while other teachers in the district are required to follow the district-adopted curriculum and materials, Aprender teachers jointly develop the curriculum and the policies and practices that support their students' learning.

Surrounding children with a team of adults who collectively possess multiple areas of expertise answers pressures from education reformers and families who advocate co-teaching to meet children's needs in general education classrooms. Beyond specific training and certifications such as special or gifted education instruction, teachers can specialise in specific subjects, technology, or the arts. In addition, a team of teachers allows children to learn from and develop relationships with multiple adults.

The new staffing model is also intended to address a key pressure facing Arizona public schools that we highlighted above: a teacher shortage exacerbated by the pandemic. By establishing a team that shared the multiple and complex responsibilities of instruction, district leaders and WUCOE partners aimed to provide student teachers and more experienced teachers with professional support. Inspired by Public Impact's Opportunity Culture initiative,[9] the teaming structure also redesigns the pipeline through the profession. The lead teacher position provides teachers with a career path intended to entice them to stay in the profession and in the classroom and provides a substantial stipend on top of an experienced teacher's salary. Thus, this position also addresses calls to elevate the teaching profession, pay teachers higher salaries, and provide a pathway to leadership for those who want to take on leadership roles–and be paid accordingly–without leaving the classroom.

### Open, flexible-use classroom space

The macrotechnical and micropolitical reforms described above were supported by another macrotechnical reform: an open, flexible, technology-enriched physical environment designed to allow teachers, students, and other adults to engage in small-group collaborative work, large group instruction, performances, and maker technology. Aprender is housed in six interconnected and reconfigured classrooms that form a 'cluster.' The cluster has a maker space at the centre, a performance space, a room dedicated to video production and podcasting, and areas for teachers and students to work in large and small groups. The furniture is moveable so the spaces can be reconfigured. The maker space has windows on all four walls which provide a 360-degree view of most areas of the cluster. Teachers facilitate learning with groups of students throughout the cluster, and students move freely as they work.

Open, flexible-use classroom spaces answer progressive education reformers' and families' pressures for learning environments that honour children's desires to move and learn by engaging in projects and hands-on activities. On their applications, the initial group of families who applied emphasised that they chose this setting because they viewed it as a strong fit for their children's learning needs. Similarly, in focus groups, participating parents highlighted the physical space and their children's opportunities for flexible movement as features of Aprender they particularly value.

### A school of choice

As a school of choice, Aprender is also a macropolitical reform. Because of the array of school choice policies in Arizona, public school districts compete with other districts, charter schools, and private schools for students. Making Aprender a school of choice addressed pressures from families and the broader policy environment to provide options for families. In Arizona, where families can easily switch schools across district boundaries because of interdistrict choice or move to the charter school sector, districts need to attract new enrollees and keep current families enrolled (Bernstein et al. 2021; Potterton 2019). Before launching Aprender, the district had to carefully advertise and market the school within the district, while managing the perception that Aprender might draw students from other district schools. The marketing plan included advertising in venues to attract students from outside the district. While there are no admissions requirements, families submit applications and, if accepted, have to enrol their children in the school.

As Aprender becomes more established, the district needs to ensure that policies are in place that prevent more privileged families from opportunity hoarding (Lewis and Diamond 2015). Innovative school choice programmes often draw the most advantaged families in the surrounding community (Sattin-Bajaj and Roda 2020). Because it emphasises self-directed learning, collaboration, technological literacy, and the organisation of work around long-term projects, the teaching and learning at Aprender tends to resemble the characteristics of managerial and professional workplaces (Bowles and Gintis 1976; Carnoy and Levin 1985; Mehta 2014). If Aprender enrols a large share of more privileged students, while other public schools that enrol less privileged students organise teaching and learning around compliance and rote learning activities such as worksheets, this dynamic can reproduce inequality. In the school's first and second years, the school's students largely mirrored the multiracial population of the district as a whole. If the number of applications submitted exceeds available seats, district staff plan to conduct a lottery where students will be selected from stratified subgroups to ensure that the enrolled students continue to match the demographics of the students enrolled in the district. As the lead teacher often states, Aprender is not a programme limited to gifted students – they take all kids. Reforms meant to expand professional opportunities for teachers and the array of learning opportunities for students should not be monopolised by advantaged families. Without broader structural and policy changes in the organisation of work and the distribution of wealth, school reforms will not be able to alter existing patterns of inequality in US society (Berliner 2006; Mehan et al. 1996). Yet districts can and should make policy choices aimed at ensuring that the reforms they undertake do not exacerbate them (Sattin-Bajaj and Roda 2020).

### *Piloting as a school-within-a-school*

Aprender embodied another micropolitical reform in that district leaders decided to launch the model as a school-within-a-school that could be scaled up rather than a full school. Because Aprender is a school of choice, district leaders aimed to address potential equity concerns from educators, families, and other community members by placing Aprender in a host school that was geographically central in the district to make it accessible to a wide range of families. They intentionally chose a host school with declining enrolment with the hopes of reversing the decline. Public school districts with enrolment decreases face budget pressures because state funding is tied to enrolment.

Aprender is ambitious in its combination of macrotechnical, micropolitical, and macropolitical reforms that embody the risks district leaders are willing to take to re-envision public schooling in a precarious environment. In this sense Aprender goes well beyond a microtechnical reform that makes modest changes in how teachers and students teach and learn without substantive organisational change. Yet as a demonstration school designed to serve a fraction of the district's 17,000 students, Aprender is a very small-scale reform. In the section below, we discuss some of the prospects for this initiative in a setting where the challenges of the pandemic have been layered on top of the already considerable challenges facing public school districts in Arizona.

## Moving from implementation to expansion

Tyack and Cuban (1995) use the term 'grammar of schooling' as shorthand for the 'established institutional forms [that have] come to be understood by educators, students, and the public as the necessary features of a 'real school': age-graded classrooms, teacher-centered instruction taught by a single teacher, curricula taught as discrete subjects, and standardised testing (86). Cuban (1993) observed that by the beginning of the twentieth century, the dominant model of instruction in US schools crystalised around the grammar of schooling. Since then, multiple waves of progressive, student-centered reforms spanning decades and district settings have faded. Because the multiple constituents of schooling have been socialised within the context of the 'real school,' its features have proven impervious to change. Reforms aimed at dramatically altering the grammar of schooling remain at the margins of schooling as specialised programmes serving a small number of students in private or public schools. While some teachers incorporate student-centered practices into their classrooms, in general, most schools and districts that attempt to reorganise schooling on a wider scale have reverted to the practices associated with the 'real school.'

In his analysis of the history of these efforts to shift instruction, Cuban (1993) observed that a key factor that can facilitate the expansion of such reforms is district support for implementation, or the extent to which district leaders provide substantive support to high profile innovations. If progressive reforms are top-down directives that are not accompanied by resources or professional development, and teachers are not involved in implementation other than being required to comply, there is likely to be little teacher buy-in. To support Aprender at the implementation phase, district leaders spent a great deal of time introducing the school through careful messaging and marketing. They revised and created new human resource policies, gave the teaching team instructional autonomy, and provided professional learning to help the teachers shift their practices. The district also incurred costs associated with remodelling the space, purchasing furniture and technology, and overstaffing the model during the first year.[10] They continue to closely monitor implementation and meet regularly with Aprender's lead teacher to address any additional support the school needs from the district. While Aprender started as a top-down initiative designed by Desert Star district leaders and their WUCOE partners, once the lead teacher was hired, district leaders gave her and the team the autonomy to develop the instructional programme and school practices around the broad design principles outlined during the design phase. The lead teacher described the latter as 'a gift given to me when I came on board' and the 'non-negotiables' for her team.

District leaders' unwavering support for Aprender bodes well for the demonstration school's survival and expansion. However, coupled with the COVID-19 pandemic, Arizona's precarious public schooling environment continues to press district leaders with multiple, and often competing, demands. These pressures might compel the most committed of educators to drift back to the grammar of schooling or traditional practices. In the next sections, we discuss these pressures and the prospects for Aprender's survival and expansion.

### Opportunities and challenges in the pandemic and beyond

While the district plans to scale up Aprender slowly to carefully balance risk-taking with navigating a precarious environment, a number of factors may hinder or facilitate Aprender's expansion. For example, district leaders considered adding another cluster at the host school for the 2020–21 school year with the goal of expanding the model more organically to the entire school. However, the pandemic foreclosed the option of creating another cluster at that time. First, safety concerns in the early stages of the pandemic precluded renovating additional physical space in the school. Second, building closures and developing plans to safely reopen consumed much of district staff members' time and energy. Instead, the school will expand to include a second cluster and sixth grade in the 2021–22 academic year.

Yet the slow pace of expansion is in tension with a micropolitical component of the model and a central goal of the initiative: reinvigorating the teaching profession by providing alternative career paths for teachers. While this goal was inspired by the precarious institutional environment for public schools in Arizona, over 45 years ago Lortie (1975) observed that teachers needed career paths to advance in the profession that would not entail leaving the classroom to become administrators. However, the pandemic has accelerated what was already an acute teacher shortage in Arizona (Arizona School Personnel Administrators Association 2020), so the slow pace of scaling up the model may not be fast enough to provide a viable solution to the teacher shortage. Similarly, even if teachers can be convinced that teaming can make their jobs easier, they might find the prospect of radically changing how they work overwhelming while trying to manage post-pandemic classrooms.

At the same time, this micropolitical component has some built in features that may help facilitate expansion. The measured pace of reform could help with buy-in among teachers at its current site and other potential sites. Additionally, the staffing model is intended to bring together an educator team with different levels of experience. Because it includes teacher candidates, the teaming structure provides teachers who are on the threshold of the profession with an apprenticeship in how to enact a teacher-led reform. The educator team can be configured in multiple ways with the long-term goal of creating additional clusters. For example, a lead teacher could pair with an experienced teacher, a novice teacher, and three full-time teacher candidates for one year in a cluster. In the following year this team could form a new cluster with one or more of the teacher candidates in the novice teacher role(s). As new clusters form, teachers should be given the latitude to re-create the model in a way that best fits their contexts with the design principles as guides (Mehan et al. 1996). Additionally, the district should provide formalised supports and professional development for new clusters. Reforms can flounder when they are dependent on the energy and commitment of the teachers implementing them rather than institutionalised practices and supports (Mehan et al. 1996).

### *Opportunities and challenges for evaluating Aprender*

The goal for Aprender's first year was to collect a range of data to assess the implementation and outcomes associated with the model. The pandemic complicated these efforts. First, the state-required accountability assessments were suspended for a year. This is a positive development for critics of accountability policies (Koretz 2017; Nichols and Berliner 2007). But it poses a dilemma for decision makers who rely on the results of state assessments as indicators of the efficacy of the model. If the students of Aprender perform less well than their peers on annual state assessments, their lower test scores could cast doubt on the school's curriculum and pedagogy. Given Arizona's competitive school choice environment, some families could unenroll their children and governing board members may feel pressured to end this experiment. District staff were keenly aware that board members would be particularly interested in the results from state assessments as they determined next steps, and that families and the broader community pay attention to test scores. As they rolled the model out to the public in the six months before the school opened, they intentionally stressed both the importance and relevance of authentic assessments (e.g. performance assessments and demonstrations) and state assessments, thus addressing high stakes accountability policies aligned with the grammar of schooling.

A second, and perhaps more relevant, indicator of success was student and family satisfaction. At the end of the 2019–20 school year, the district surveyed families and students, asking them to reflect on their experiences with Aprender before schools closed for in-person instruction. The 52 parents (69%) who responded overwhelmingly reported that their children were engaged and enjoyed going to school. Similarly, most (78%) of the 41 students who responded reported that they were excited to go to school often or all of the time. These results are promising given that they were surveyed two months after schools in Arizona physically closed because of the pandemic. The district continues to formally and informally survey parents and students about their experiences with Aprender as it moves forward with expansion.

A third indicator of the model's success is if the families from Aprender's first year re-enrolled their students for the following year and if new students enrolled. Sixty-one, or 81%, of the students who were enrolled in 2019–20 re-enrolled in 2020–21, along with 51 new students which brought the school to just under capacity in its second year.[11] Because the pandemic upended many families' schooling plans, this drop in enrolment may not be an assessment of the model per se, but could have been driven by families' needs during the pandemic. Similarly, some students' responses to open-ended questions on the student survey suggested that Aprender may not be a good fit for students who need a more structured educational environment. Given its small size, a handful of students leaving the school is large in percentage terms.

A fourth indicator of success is the extent to which the five design principles are actualised. We conducted interviews and classroom observations to help district leaders understand how implementation was proceeding and what additional supports they

## 116     EDUCATIONAL LEADERSHIP AND POLICY IN A TIME OF PRECARITY

could provide. The parent and student surveys tapped into the five design principles and helped teachers identify some areas of need, such as more frequent and effective communication with parents. District leaders and WUCOE partners found that creating a transformative learning space was the easiest aspect to implement (Cuban 1993). Student-centered learning and the team of educators presented some challenges, and district leaders continue to learn how to support them. Because district leaders focused on these three design principles when the school launched, district staff were less attentive to the design principles of equity and inclusion and a culture of care, community, and collaboration. However, these design principles are reflected in the teachers' work at the school level.

## Conclusion

As we reflect on how these district leaders chose to take risks and champion Aprender, we draw two lessons that can help leaders in other settings enact and nurture ambitious school reforms while navigating similarly precarious environments. First, leaders need to give themselves time throughout the design and implementation phases to balance what are often competing interests and pressures on public education, including during a crisis. Aprender's district leaders and WUCOE partners spent more than two years designing Aprender, and continue to carefully monitor implementation. Aprender's design combined a unique set of macrotechnical, micropolitical, and macropolitical reforms aimed at addressing the precarious institutional environment for public schools in Arizona: underfunding, a teacher shortage, and the aggressive privatisation and marketisation policies enacted by the state legislature. District leaders and WUCOE partners continue to reflect on how to negotiate the multitude of pressures the school faces, both during the pandemic and beyond. At the same time, this measured pace aimed at building support for their efforts within the district may not be sufficient to address the challenges posed by the dynamic political environment for public schools and districts that we described at the outset of this paper. Second, to expand or scale up Aprender, district leaders need to balance providing substantive support for implementation and granting teachers the autonomy to adapt the model to address their sites and students' needs.

This paper describes how in the process of designing and implementing Aprender, district leaders attempted to balance politically oppositional demands on public education, which in turn has implications for how Aprender can survive and expand. Aprender is a high-profile innovation that is highly supported by district leaders, whose measured pace of design, implementation, and expansion is helping them navigate their precarious environment. While this process is not without its tensions, we see Aprender as a bellwether for public education in Arizona more generally, and a model that points the way to how educational leaders might respond to some of the existential challenges facing public schools in the US and other highly marketised educational settings in the wake of the pandemic and beyond.

## Notes

1. Rather than a coherent political agenda, neoliberalism is an ensemble of theoretical arguments and policies focused on dismantling social welfare policies and extending the reach

of market discourse and practices into social life (Carvalho and Rodrigues 2006; Harvey 2005).

2. We use the term 'demonstration school' because district leaders see Aprender as a site for testing innovative structures and practices with the goal of expanding them to other sites.
3. Between 2008 and 2014, Arizona's state funding for public education decreased by 23%, making it the US state with the largest cuts to education during the recession when its funding for education was among the lowest of US states (Leachman et al. 2016).
4. The names of the school, district, and university are pseudonyms.
5. Our role as researchers is an extension of the partnership between the school district and the WUCOE that started during the design process.
6. Here, we use the term 'state' to denote the broad array of US federal, state, and local educational agencies involved in the funding, regulation, and provision of public education.
7. In 2017–18, Arizona's public school students were 38% white, 46% Latinx, 5% Black, 5% American Indian, 3% Asian American, and 3% were multi-racial.
8. While the curriculum and pedagogy for the school is teacher-driven, the teachers draw upon the Buck Institute for Education's vision and resources for project-based learning (https://www.pblworks.org). Recent studies suggest that project-based learning improves students' academic and social and emotional outcomes (Duke et al. 2021; Krajcik et al. 2021).
9. For more information, see www.opportunityculture.org.
10. Although Aprender was under capacity in its first year at 75 students when it could enrol 120, it was overstaffed to allow the teachers to develop the model and get the school started.
11. Enrolment in the district dropped by about 7% from 2019–20 to 2020–21. The district created a new fully online school to accommodate families needs during the pandemic and keep students enrolled in the district.

## Acknowledgements

We would like to thank the leaders and staff of Desert Star and Aprender for their support of this project.

## Disclosure statement

No potential conflict of interest was reported by the author(s).

## ORCID

*Jeanne M. Powers* ⓘ http://orcid.org/0000-0001-5197-6546
*Lok-Sze Wong* ⓘ http://orcid.org/0000-0003-4017-6783

## References

Arizona Department of Revenue. 2020. *School Tuition Organisation Income Tax Credits in Arizona: Summary of Activity FY2018/19.* https://azdor.gov/sites/default/files/media/REPORTS_CREDITS_2020_fy2019-private-school-tuition-org-credit-report.pdf.

Arizona School Personnel Administrators Association. 2019. *Human Resources Professionals in Arizona Schools.* December. https://azednews.com/severe-teacher-shortage-in-arizona-continues-3/.

Arizona School Personnel Administrators Association. 2020. *Human Resources Professionals in Arizona Schools.* August 31. https://ewscripps.brightspotcdn.com/71/d9/c6e0a05c487fb362d17df52ec5bd/aspaa-pressrelease-09-17-20-2.pdf.

Ball, S. J. 2013. *The Education Debate.* 2nd ed. Bristol: The Polity Press.

Bauerlein, V., and Y. Koh. 2020. "Teacher Shortage Compounds COVID-19 Crisis in Schools." *Wall Street Journal,* December 15. https://www.wsj.com/articles/teacher-shortage-compounds-covid-crisis-in-schools-11608050176.

Berger, R., L. Woodfin, and A. Vilen. 2016. *Learning That Lasts: Challenging, Engaging, and Empowering Students with Deeper Instruction.* New York, NY: Wiley.

Berliner, D. C. 2006. "Our Impoverished View of Educational Research." *Teachers College Record* 108 (6): 949–995. https://www.tcrecord.org/Content.asp?ContentId=12106.

Bernstein, K. A., A. Alvarez, S. Chaparro, and K. I. Henderson. 2021. "'We Live in the Age of Choice': School Administrators, School Choice Policies, and the Shaping of Dual Language Bilingual Education." *Language Policy,* 1–30. doi:10.1007/s10993-021-09578-0.

Bowles, S., and H. Gintis. 1976. *Schooling in Capitalist America.* New York, NY: Basic Books.

Carnoy, M., and H. M. Levin. 1985. *Schooling and Work in the Democratic State.* Stanford, CA: Stanford University Press.

Carvalho, L. F., and J. Rodrigues. 2006. "On Markets and Morality: Revisiting Fred Hirsch." *Review of Social Economy* 64 (3): 331–348. doi:10.1080/00346760600892758.

Center for Budget and Policy Priorities. 2020. "States Grappling with Hit to Tax Collections." *State budget watch,* November 6. https://www.cbpp.org/research/state-budget-and-tax/states-start-grappling-with-hit-to-tax-collections.

Center for Education Reform. 2021. *National Charter School Law Rankings and Scorecard.* https://edreform.com/issues/choice-charter-schools/laws-legislation/.

Corcoran, T., and M. Goertz. 2005. "The Governance of Public Education." In *The Public Schools,* edited by S. Fuhrman, and M. Lazerson, 25–56. New York, NY: Oxford University Press.

Cuban, L. 1993. *How Teachers Taught.* New York, NY: Teachers College Press.

Dewey, J. 1938. *Experience and Education.* New York, NY: Simon & Schuster.

Dewey, J. 2017. *School and Society.* Project Gutenberg, January 7. https://www.gutenberg.org/ebooks/53910.

Duke, N. K., A.-L. Halvorsen, S. L. Strachan, J. Kim, and S. Konstantopoulos. 2021. "Putting PjBL to the Test: The Impact of Project-Based Learning on Second Graders' Social Studies and Literacy Learning and Motivation in low-ses School Settings." *American Educational Research Journal* 58 (1): 160–200. doi:10.3102/0002831220929638.

García, E. 2020. "The Pandemic Sparked More Appreciation for Teachers, but Will It Give Them a Voice in Education and Their Working Conditions?" *Working Economics Blog,* May 7. https://www.epi.org/blog/the-pandemic-sparked-more-appreciation-for-teachers-but-will-it-give-them-a-voice-in-education-and-their-working-conditions/.

Harris, C. 2018. "Lawmaker Eddie Farnsworth Nets $13.9 Million in Charter School Sale, Keeps Getting Paid." *Arizona Republic,* November 28. https://www.azcentral.com/story/news/local/

arizona-education/2018/11/28/farnsworth-net-13-9-million-benjamin-franklin-charter-school-sale/2126183002/.

Harvey, D. 2005. *A Brief History of Neoliberalism*. New York, NY: Oxford University Press.

Hussar, B., J. Zhang, S. Hein, K. Wang, A. Roberts, J. Cui, M. Smith, F. B. Mann, A. Barmer, and R. Dilig. 2020. *The Condition of Education 2020 (NCES 2020-144)*. Washington, DC: National Center for Education Statistics. https://nces.ed.gov/pubs2020/2020144.pdf.

Koretz, D. 2017. *The Testing Charade: Pretending to Make Schools Better*. Chicago, IL: University of Chicago Press.

Krajcik, J., B. Schneider, E. Miller, I-C. Chen, L. Bradford, K. Bartz, Q. Baker, A. Palinscar, D. Peak-Brown, and S. Codere. 2021. *Assessing the Effect of Project-Based Learning on Science Learning in Elementary Schools*. Michigan State University Create for STEM Institute. https://mlpbl.open3d.science/techreport.

Labaree, D. F. 1997. "Public Goods, Private Goods: The American Struggle Over Educational Goals." *American Educational Research Journal* 34 (1): 39–81. doi:10.3102/00028312034001039.

Labaree, D. F. 2010. "How Dewey Lost: The Victory of David Snedden and Social Efficiency in the Reform of American Education." In *Pragmatism and Modernities*, edited by D. Tröhler, T. Schlag, and F. Osterwalder, 163–188. Brill Sense. https://doi.org/10.1163/9789460913457_011.

Lake, R. 2019. "Preparing Students for the Uncertain Future." *The 74*, March 27. https://www.the74million.org/article/preparing-students-for-the-uncertain-future-why-americas-educators-are-ready-to-innovate-but-their-education-systems-are-not/.

Leachman, M. 2019. *K-12 Funding Still Lagging in Many States*. May 29. Center for Budget and Policy Priorities. https://www.cbpp.org/blog/k-12-funding-still-lagging-in-many-states.

Leachman, M., N. Albares, K. Masterson, and M. Wallace. 2016. *Most States Have Cut School Funding, and Some Continue Cutting*. January 25. Center for Budget and Policy Priorities. http://www.cbpp.org/research/state-budget-and-tax/most-states-have-cut-school-funding-and-some-continue-cutting.

Lewis, A., and J. Diamond. 2015. *Despite the Best Intentions: How Racial Inequality Thrives in Schools*. New York, NY: Oxford University Press.

Lortie, D. 1975. *Schoolteacher: A Sociological Study*. Chicago, IL: University of Chicago Press.

Mehan, H., I. Villanueva, L. Hubbard, and A. Lintz. 1996. *Constructing School Success: The Consequences of Untracking Low-Achieving Students*. New York, NY: Cambridge University Press.

Mehta, J. 2013. *The Allure of Order*. New York, NY: Oxford University Press.

Mehta, J. 2014. "Deeper Learning Has a Race Problem." *Education Week*, June 20. https://www.edweek.org/leadership/opinion-deeper-learning-has-a-race-problem/2014/06.

Millar, K. M. 2017. "Toward a Critical Politics of Precarity." *Sociology Compass* 11 (6): e12483. doi:10.1111/soc4.12483.

Minow, M. 2010. *In Brown's Wake: Legacies of America's Educational Landmark*. New York, NY: Oxford University Press.

National Science Board. 2020. Expenditures per Pupil for Elementary and Secondary Public Schools (dollars). https://ncses.nsf.gov/indicators/states/indicator/public-school-per-pupil-expenditures/table.

Nichols, S., and D. Berliner. 2007. *Collateral Damage: How High-Stakes Testing Corrupts America's Schools*. Cambridge, MA: Harvard Education Press.

Peters, M. A. 2012. "Postmodern Educational Capitalism, Global Information Systems and new Media Networks." *Policy Futures in Education* 10 (1): 23–29. doi:10.2304/pfie.2012.10.1.23.

Potterton, A. U. 2019. "Power, Influence, and Policy in Arizona's Education Market: "We've Got to out-Charter the Charters"." *Power and Education* 11 (3): 291–308. doi:10.1177/1757743818816712.

Powers, J. M. 2009. *Charter Schools: From Reform Imagery to Reform Reality*. New York, NY: Palgrave Macmillan.

Reese, W. J. 2005. *America's Public Schools: From the Common School to No Child Left Behind*. Baltimore, MD: Johns Hopkins University Press.

Sattin-Bajaj, C., and A. Roda. 2020. "Opportunity Hoarding in School Choice Contexts: The Role of Policy Design in Promoting Middle-Class Parents' Exclusionary Behaviors." *Educational Policy* 34 (7): 992–1035. doi:10.1177/0895904818802106.

Semel, S. 1999. "Introduction." In *'Schools of Tomorrow,' Schools of Today: What Happened to Progressive Education*, edited by S. F. Semel, and A. R. Sadovnik, 1–20. New York, NY: Peter Lang.

Standing, G. 2014. *A Precariat Charter: From Denizens to Citizens*. Bloomsbury Academic. http://dx.doi.org/10.5040/9781472510631.ch-002.

Tyack, D., and L. Cuban. 1995. *Tinkering Toward Utopia: A Century of Public School Reform*. Cambridge, MA: Harvard University Press.

Whitty, G. (1997). Creating Quasi-Markets in Education: A Review of Recent Research on Parental Choice and School Autonomy in Three Countries. *Review of Research in Education 22:* 3–47.

Will, M., C. Gewertz, and S. Schwartz. 2020. "Did COVID-19 Really Drive Teachers to Quit?" *Education Week*, November 10. https://www.edweek.org/ew/issues/teacher-retirements/teachers-said-covid-19-would-drive-them-to.html.

# Index

Note: **Bold** page numbers refer to tables; *Italic* page numbers refer to figures and page numbers followed by "n" denote endnotes.

academy/academic: capitalism 37; gig academy 39; mainstream primary school 79; managerial relationships 38–40; multi-academy trusts 70; neoliberalism 37–38; workforce positions 40
accountability 4, 69, 80, 92
adolescent career identity 10
Alberti, Gabriella 1
analytic approach 41
Angel, K. 72
apprenticeship 114
Aprender: demonstration school 109; implementation to expansion 113–114; open, flexible-use classroom space 111; opportunities and challenges 115–116; progressive curriculum and pedagogies 109–110; school of choice 111–112; school-within-a-school 112–113; team of educators 110–111
Archer, John 39
Arizona 105; to fund public schools 106; neoliberal education policies 107; public schooling environment 106; public school students 106
Australia: casualised work rate 8; compulsory schooling 10; Cultural and Creative Industries 21; lowpaid employment 9; secondary school students 3; unemployment or under-employment 8; unemployment/under-employment 8
authentic individuality 45
autonomy, school leaders 79

Bachelor of Creative Industries Program (BCI) 22, 24
Bailey, S. 3
Ballet, K. 72
Barnett, R. 22–24, 30–31
Bauer, S. 71
Beatty, B. R. 70
Beck, V. 58

Berkovich, I. 71
Boler, M. 70
Boulton, D. 90
Bourdieu, P. 85, 87, 93, 97
Boxenbaum, E. 88
Braun, A. 88
Bridgstock, R. 23
broader employment relationship 39
Brotherton, G. 72
Brown, A. 90
*Brown v. Board of Education* 108
Bullough, R. V. 72

Campbell, Marie 41
career development learning (CDL) 23
careers 8–9; in Australian schools 9–10; decision-making 8; education 10; identity crisis 10; insecurity 14; malleability 14, 15; management skills 23, 25; planning abilities 11
care, ethic of 45–47
Carnoy, M. 108, 109
casual employment 8, 38, 55, 56, 60, 63, 65
casualisation 7, 55
Casual Teachers Award 55
challenges, school leaders 75–76
Chief Investigators (CIs) 40
citizenship 21, 22
cohesion 1
Collinson, J. A. 39
competitive employment markets 9
compulsory schooling, Australia 10
consumer dupes 11
consumerism morality 85
consumers empowerment 85
Covid-19 pandemic 2, 3, 4, 5, 8; data analysis 75; economic impacts of 8; English school system 69–70; far-reaching effects of 105; methodology 73–81; opportunities and challenges 114; precarity, isolation and vulnerability 70–71; sample 74–75; school

# INDEX

leaders 69; student learning at university 28; WhatsApp group 78
Crawford, M. 82
creative activity 31n1
creative industries (CI) 21; graduate employability 23; higher education role 22–24; portfolio careers 25
Crimmins, Gail 3
critical vulnerability 73
critique, ethic of 47–48
Cuban, L. 113
Cuckoo lens 92–93
cultural activity 31n1
curriculum design 25–26; graduate employability 25–26; implications for 30–31; to support the lifeworld 29–30

Dale, M. 73
data analysis 42
decision-making 14, 110
della Porta, Donatella 2
democracy 1
Desert Star School District 107, 113
digital profile 27
discipline-appropriate profile/portfolio format 27
Divan, Aysha 22
*doxa* and *illusio* 88, 97

Ecclestone, K. 71
Edgar, Susan 23
educational systems 1; educational leadership 2; education reform 4–5; government policy 23; marketisation of 21; precarious employment 1
educators, two-tier system 2
Egdell, V. 58
emancipatory paradigm 29
emotional experiences 70
emotional wellbeing 82
employability 20; behaviours 13; concept of 23; of graduates 21, 22; higher education 23; individualist turn 23
employees 37
employment 8–9; gender and age 65; landscapes 15, 54; markets 9, 12; opportunities 8; policy 54; post-education 10; status and work demands **61**; teaching experience **63**; textually-mediated social interaction 43
Empowerment Scholarship Accounts (ESA) 107
English local authorities (LAs) 71
entrepreneurialism 14
Entwistle, Lewis 4
ethical leadership 38, 41, 42
ethical responsibilities 4
extra-curricular activities 12, 13
extrinsic job quality 57
Eyal, O. 71

Facebook 26–27
'feminised' profession 65
Fielding, M. 92
Fitzgerald, Scott 4
fixed-term contract teaching work 54, 56
fixed-term employment 57–58
flexibility 9
Frye, E. M. 73
Further Education (FE) sector 85

game-changing 96–98
game-player metaphor 85
Gavin, Mihajla 4
gender 11, 30
Gergen, K. J. 91
Gibson, W. 90
gig academy 39
gig economy 1, 2
Ginsberg, R. 70
Gleeson, Joanne 3
global economic conditions 8
global education reform movement (GERM) 85–87
global employment landscapes 10
Goff, Mhorag 3
Good Universities Guide 25
government policies 20
graduate employability 20, 22, 25–26
graduate unemployment 20
grammar of schooling 113
Gray Davies, T. 70
Gregor, Frances 41
Griffith, Alison I. 41
Gunter, H. M. 88, 93, 96

Habermas, J. 3, 21, 23, 24, 29, 31
Hammersley, M. 90
Harness, Oliver 4
Harris, Jess 3
Hartley, D. 92
higher education (HE) 1, 3, 8, 20, 21, 23
Higher Education Act 89
Hillvale Project 85
homo promptus 11, 12, 15; career identity 14; concept of 7–8; uncertainty and contingency 13
Howard, M. P. 71

Importance of Teaching (DfE) 69
individualist turn 23
inequality 25, 108, 112
inequity 1, 42
inquiry 2, 31, 38, 41, 88
insecurity 2, 5, 7, 14, 43, 56, 93
'inspirational' leadership models 73
institutional ethnography 41

## INDEX

inter-organisational mobility 9
intrinsic job quality 57, 60, 62, 63

Jackson, Denise A. 23
Jenkins, K. 57
job prospects 57, 62
job satisfaction 39
job status congruence 57
Jopling, Michael 4
justice, ethic of 43–45

Kelchtermans, G. 72, 82
Kelly, P. 11
knowledge workers 20
Kofman, Yelizavetta 1

labour conditions 2
labour flexibility policies 22
labour markets 8; lowpaid employment 9;
    segmentation 58
leadership effectiveness 70
Lee, Ching Kwan Lee 1
Lee, Louise 39
lens: of game-changing 96–98; of powerful
    gameplay 93–94; of precarious gameplay
    94–95; re-focusing 98–99; of therapeutic
    gameplay 95–96
Levin, H. M. 108, 109
LinkedIn 27
Lipton, Briony 3
'little-p' policy 105
Lizzio, Alf 27
local authority (LA) oversight 69
'Local Schools, Local Decisions' (LSLD)
    reform 56
Lock and Key lens 91
Loughlin, C. 58
lowpaid employment 9
low socio-economic status (LSES) 25
low-trust organisation culture 85

macrotechnical reforms 108, 111
Maguire, M. 88
make merit-based selection 56
Mallory, B. J. 71
Mantelpiece lens 92
market economies 22
Mauri, Christian 49
Mavers, D. 90
Maxwell, T. 57
McCormack, A. 56
McGrath-Champ, Susan 4
McIntyre, Joanna 3
McVarish, J. 71
mental health and wellbeing 82
mental health implications 39

merit selection process 65
metaphorical lenses: Cuckoo lens 92–93; Lock
    and Key lens 91; Mantelpiece lens 92; Welcome
    Mat lens 91–92
micropolitical reform 110, 112
micro-political struggles 72
Millar, K. M. 1, 2
Mooi-Reci, I. 65
Morgan, G. 25
Morrison, M. 71
multi-academy trusts (MATs) 69
multi-disciplinary curriculum 109
Murray, R. 58

National Employer Satisfaction Survey 26
Nelligan, P. 25
neoliberal education policies 106, 107
neoliberal education policy reforms 4
neoliberalism 23, 37–38, 69, 105
New South Wales (NSW) 54; public school
    teachers 54; public sector teachers' union 55;
    temporary employment 61
Nikunen, Minna 40
non-tenured researchers (NTRs) 38; ethical
    leadership 42–43; ethic of care 45–47; ethic
    of critique 47–48; ethic of justice 43–45;
    managerial relationships 38; relative paucity
    42; social relationships 42
non-traditional learner 26–27
normative behaviour 13
NSW Teachers' Federation (NSWTF) 59

opportunity gaps 1
Ortenblad, A. 88

Pajo, Karl 39
Percy, Alisa 39
performance-measurement technologies 87
permanent contracts 38
permanent employment 57
Peters, M. 11
Piot, L. 72
portfolio careers 25
positive working relationship 44
post-pandemic times 9
post-school employment market 10
post-school lives 7, 8
post-school tertiary education pathways 8
post-school transitions 9
Potter, T. 72
powerful gameplay 93–94
Powers, Jeanne M. 4
precarious employment 1–2; education workers
    experiences 3–4; labour conditions 3–4; scope
    and visibility of 2
precarious gameplay 94–95

precarity concept 2
precarity notions 1
pressure, school leaders 76–77
pressurised environments 3–4
Preston, B. 57, 58, 63, 66
primary labour markets 57
professional development plan 27
proxy-employers 49
public communication skills 29
public education: Aprender, a demonstration school 109; conceptual framework 108; marketisation and deregulation of 107; multiple pressures 109–113
public school teachers 54, 58
public-sector employees 25
public sphere 85
Putnam, L. 88

radical responsibilisation 40
Rayner, S. M. 88, 93
Reese, W. J. 110
regular support/supervision 78–79
Restorick, J. 90
rethinking schools: rethinking accountability 80; technology supporting change 80–81
Rosa, H. 15
Rose, N. 11
Rouleau, L. 88
Ruck Simmonds, M. 73, 82

Salvatore, J. 71
Schechter, C. 88
school-based careers education 8, 15
school choice programmes 112
school leaders 8, 42; autonomy 79; challenges 75–76; human impact on 69; performance-based contracts for 1; pressure 76–77; regular support/supervision 78–79; support 77–78; temporary teaching 64
school 'self-improvement' 69
secondary labour markets 57
self-enterprise 12
short-term teaching contracts 1
Skeggs, Beverley 21
skills, qualities and connections audit 27
Smith, Dorothy E. 41
Smithers, Kathleen 3
Smith, H. 57
social inequality 108
social inquiry 41
social media platform 26
social welfare policies 117n1
socioeconomic status 11
socio-political priorities 21
soft money 40
Somekh, B. 90
Spina, Nerida 3

Stacey, Meghan 4
Standing, G. 87
Starratt, R. J. 38, 41, 43
Stephenson, L. 71
Steward, J. 71
Strongly Disagree – Strongly Agree 10
student employability 22–24
student-to-adult ratio 110
study-career aspirations 11
supercomplexity 22–24; as epistemological hinterland 23
supplementary material 11
systemic sustainable policy 39

Tahir, L. 71
'tasks of criticism' process 23, 29
teachers 8; education pathways 9; on fixedterm contracts 56; inadequate knowledge 10; make merit-based selection 56; in NSW public schools 55; on short-term contracts 2; in temporary employment 55; workforce 55
teaching: 'feminised' profession 65; workforce 1
technology supporting change 80–81
temporary teaching 54, 55; employment category 59; explorations of 55; fixed-term employment 57–58; implications 65–66; in research literature 56–57; and school leadership 62–65; workload in 59–62
tenuous periphery 45
therapeutic gameplay 95–96
Thomas, K. 56
Threadgold, S. 11
Tilbury, Fiona 40
Tomaszewski, Wojtek 23
Townsend, A. 91
Trehan, K. 88
Twitter 40
Tyack, D. 113

unemployment/under-employment 8, 58
university-licensed Qualtrics-based online survey 10
University of the Sunshine Coast (USC) 24
unworthiness 91
US educational system 106

Victorian Department of Education 10
video series 28
de Villiers Scheepers, Margarietha 3
vulnerability theories 69; approaching and embracing 71–73; definitions of 71
vulnerability zeitgeist 71

Walsh, Lucas 3
Web 2.0 27
Welcome Mat lens 91–92

Western University College of Education (WUCOE) 107
Wilson, Keithia 27
Wilson, Rachel 4
Wong, Lok-Sze 4
Wooden, M. 65
Wood, J. 25
Woods, P. 92

work experience 12
workforce environments 1
working time quality 57, 60
work-integrated learning (WIL) initiatives 28–29
workload in temporary teaching 59–62

Zepke, Nick 23
Zorn, D. 70

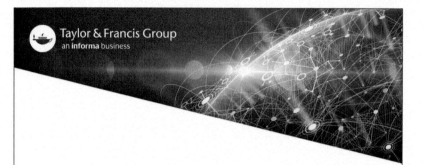

# Taylor & Francis eBooks

www.taylorfrancis.com

A single destination for eBooks from Taylor & Francis with increased functionality and an improved user experience to meet the needs of our customers.

90,000+ eBooks of award-winning academic content in Humanities, Social Science, Science, Technology, Engineering, and Medical written by a global network of editors and authors.

### TAYLOR & FRANCIS EBOOKS OFFERS:

- A streamlined experience for our library customers
- A single point of discovery for all of our eBook content
- Improved search and discovery of content at both book and chapter level

## REQUEST A FREE TRIAL
support@taylorfrancis.com

Gail Crimmins [ID], Briony Lipton, Joanna McIntyre [ID], Margarietha de Villiers Scheepers [ID] and Peter English

62 EDUCATIONAL LEADERSHIP AND POLICY IN A TIME OF PRECARITY

78    EDUCATIONAL LEADERSHIP AND POLICY IN A TIME OF PRECARITY

# EDUCATIONAL LEADERSHIP AND POLICY IN A TIME OF PRECARITY

96    EDUCATIONAL LEADERSHIP AND POLICY IN A TIME OF PRECARITY

## EDUCATIONAL LEADERSHIP AND POLICY IN A TIME OF PRECARITY 113

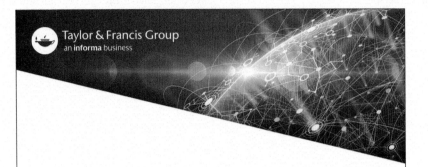